The Crisis of Dependency

How Our Efforts to Solve Poverty Are Trapping People in It and What We Can Do to Foster Freedom Instead

JAMES WHITFORD

The Crisis of Dependency
Copyright © 2024 by James Whitford
All rights reserved.

Published in the United States of America by Credo House Publishers,
a division of Credo Communications LLC, Grand Rapids, Michigan
credohousepublishers.com

ISBN: 978-1-62586-289-1

Cover and interior design by Jonathan Lewis
Editing by Bellwether Communications and Nycole Sinks

Printed in the United States of America
First Edition

Whitford's new book both inspires and challenges us: If we don't get the nature of the person right, even our most generous and well-intended actions will fail to lift the poor out of poverty. By contrast, *The Crisis of Dependency* shows how everyone can claim their birthright of dignity, hope, and freedom.

—**Kris Mauren**, President and Cofounder, Acton Institute

James Whitford is a man on a mission—actually, *two* missions. One is to help people who need and deserve assistance. The other, every bit as important, is to teach his fellow Americans there are both right ways and wrong ways to go about it. This is the book every true humanitarian has been waiting for.

—**Lawrence W. Reed**, president emeritus, Foundation for Economic Education

James Whitford is one of the most strategic, compassionate, and instructive leaders I have ever met. Rather than just quantify the problem of homelessness and poverty, he offers a roadmap to solutions—including roles and responsibilities for each of us to fulfill and how to leverage the power of freedom and accountability. This book will change your life, make you a better person, and enable you to be a more powerful asset in your community.

—**Tarren Bragdon**, President and CEO, Foundation for Government Accountability

In a combination of heart-felt storytelling, first-hand experience and, most importantly, solutions that work, *The Crisis of Dependency* will reframe our decades of poverty failures. It gives us practical advice we can use to expand freedom for everyone.

—**Matt Paprocki**, President and CEO, Illinois Policy Institute

James underscores a well-informed and thoughtful approach to inspiring freedom and not just charity. The quick-hitting antidotes and personal stories in this book connect the dots for real-time, real-life change. In a sedulous moment of divine tension in our world, we must journey toward inspiring people to choose freedom and not the status quo. *The Crisis of Dependency* will certainly move you toward the former more than the latter.

—**Dr. Wayman Ming**, Jr., General Bishop, Pentecostal Church of God

Whitford's wealth of personal experience empowering downtrodden neighbors to emerge from poverty paints a stark picture: our current public programs are imprisoning people in dependency. I want stacks of this book to hand out to every faith-based charity and government bureaucrat I meet.

—**Rachel Ferguson,** Director, Free Enterprise Center at Concordia University Chicago and author of *Black Liberation Through the Marketplace: Hope, Heartbreak, and the Promise of America*

The Crisis of Dependency is a clarion call emphasizing that many current efforts to solve poverty often create dependency rather than fostering independence. Whitford tells us that we are overdue to pick up the mantle of caring for the poor and return it to "the shoulders of compassionate neighbors, corner churches, and local ministries."

—**Ed Kornegay, PhD,** Executive Director, Center for Poverty Solutions, Illinois Policy Institute

With a heart of compassion that gets to the heart of the matter, Whitford brings together faith and philanthropy, responsibility and relationship to overcome the arguments and actions that keep people in bondage. *The Crisis of Dependency* will provide a breakthrough in your thinking so you can move away from perpetuating dependency to charity that achieves real freedom.

—**Tom De Vries,** President and CEO, Citygate Network

Contents

Foreword — vii

Introduction — 1

CHAPTER 1: Charity and Justice — 7

CHAPTER 2: Independence and Freedom — 17

CHAPTER 3: Empowerment — 31

CHAPTER 4: Charity Displaced — 49

CHAPTER 5: Relationships Displaced — 61

INTERLUDE: The Parable of Iustitia — 75

CHAPTER 6: The Heart — 81

CHAPTER 7: Smart Practice — 89

CHAPTER 8: Wise Philanthropy — 99

CHAPTER 9: Embracing Policy — 107

Conclusion — 117

Challenge Questions — 121

Acknowledgments — 129

References — 131

Foreword

Marvin Olasky

HILLSDALE COLLEGE IN MICHIGAN IS honored by conservatives and disliked by liberals for many reasons, but among them is its refusal of any government aid since the 1980s. No federally funded research grants for professors. No Pell Grants or other government dollars for students. Hillsdale is loud and proud regarding the reasons for its stance: "Our independence allows us to maintain the integrity of our classical liberal arts curriculum, and to remain true to our founding mission of providing an education to 'all persons who wish, irrespective of nationality, color, or sex.'"

As a journalist, I've seen how many Christian groups fighting homelessness also turn down government money, but even those that do so often rely on participants using SNAP cards—a.k.a. food stamps—and other federal payments such as SSI (supplemental security income). Until recently, I didn't know of any programs pursuing the radical notion that clients capable of working should give up their SNAP benefits not only when they earn enough to become ineligible, but while they are still eligible.

That's just what Watered Gardens in Joplin, Missouri, proposes, and it's what James Whitford expounds on in this book. James and Marsha Whitford started Watered Gardens in 2000. The name comes from chapter 58 of Isaiah: "The Lord will guide you continually . . . You shall be like a watered garden, like a spring of water, whose waters do not fail." At first glance, the website's statistical summary of last year's efforts is like that of many other shelters: "29,437 needs met." But next to it is an unusual stat—"70 percent needs *earned*"—and one even rarer: "46,470 pounds *earned*" (emphasis added).

The Watered Gardens philosophy is that all who are capable of work should earn their room and board, not be given it. James Whitford previously worked as a physical therapist who specialized in wound therapy. He brings that training to his ministry's moral therapy: "As a wound care specialist with a decade of practice, I know that simply covering a serious wound with a mere bandage can complicate the problem, resulting in a deeper infection or an abscess." A roof over a person's head is just a big Band-Aid unless it comes with relationship (every person is meant to be with another) and redemption (every person is meant to be with God).

Sometimes, as Whitford notes in this book, patients who need painful moments to bring about healing call their physical therapists "physical terrorists." Whitford pushes residents to be all they can be, and they don't want to disappoint him. Those who have become dependent on SNAP benefits don't like giving them up, but a wall at Watered Gardens alongside a coffee pot displays the forty-three SNAP cards residents have voluntarily turned over. Whitford doesn't know what's happened to twenty-six of the people who once relied on those cards, but he has information on seventeen. Three have fallen back into SNAP, four have died, and ten have stayed independent.

I've interviewed one of the independents, Barry Meyer, and plan to interview more. Meyer, nearly fifty years old in 2018 and still strong, was "working, doing good, thinking, 'I qualify by government standards but don't really need 'em.' I'd rag on people that did what I was doing: 'Why are you taking advantage? Do it on your own.' I was thinking, 'Man, you're a hypocrite, ragging on people for doing something you're doing.'" So Meyer handed over his SNAP Card to Whitford, trusting in "God's providing."

Will other shelters take on the challenge of turning down government money and suggesting to clients that they do the same? Whitford is trying to take the Watered Gardens way nationwide by developing a True Charity Initiative. He tells about his experience and goals in this book. Some say higher education in the US is a hopeless mess, but when I spoke and met students at Hillsdale, I came away hopeful. My visit to Joplin left me similarly optimistic.

This book not only shows optimism but offers practical ways to make those hopes a reality. Readers of this book will learn how we can move forward in an area that drives many to despair. With the right support and motivation, many programs and thousands of able-bodied people can, like Meyer, give up dependence on government and resolve to work hard and depend on God.

Introduction

LIKE MOST PEOPLE, I LIVE in a home with a shower that provides hot running water, reliable electricity, a well-stocked kitchen, and an attic full of memorabilia and seasonal décor. Like many others, I also enjoy a life filled with a wide array of choices: options for what to eat, different types of recreation, and various vacation destinations. Adding a high-paced, purposeful career makes for a very full life.

Yet, amid our everyday busy lives, we often overlook the little things: lost or discarded items on the roadside, coins on the sidewalk, clean water from a sink, even access to soap. It's easy to grow accustomed to these conveniences, failing to value them—until one day, I could no longer take them for granted.

I learned how those little things appear to a homeless person. Change on the curb was genuine money. Litter on the road—well, one man's trash is another man's treasure, and many homeless individuals collect such treasures. The hands of the clock crawl by when you have no home to clean or television to watch. The deep stench is hard to beat, the sourness that penetrates your skin no matter how hard you try to stay clean.

At this point, it had been seven years since my wife and I founded our mission, Watered Gardens Ministries, in southwest Missouri. After spending years with homeless people, I began to feel a strange sensation that I should leave my house and wander the streets. Most sound and reasonable people would quickly push the thought aside. So I did. It came again and again, but I ignored it over and over.

Eventually, there was no avoiding it. I sat down with my wife to tell her. What a tough conversation that was! Imagine telling your spouse that you believe God is telling you to leave her and your five children for a season to go live on the streets. As expected, she didn't take too kindly to the idea and sharply countered, "I think God will tell me if you're going to go live on the streets!" End of conversation.

That night we opened a book we had been reading together, *Crazy Love* by Francis Chan. The opening story was about a man who voluntarily lived on the streets with the homeless. I read a few sentences before the silence overtook us, and I saw a tear run down her face.

The next day, in mid-November, I left with nothing but the clothes on my back.

One evening during this short stint of existing outside, I ran into Ralph. Ralph was a young man in his mid-twenties who had struggled with chronic homelessness. He was thin and blue-eyed with a mass of curly, sandy blond hair. I always thought he looked like someone who belonged on a beach with a surfboard under his arm. I knew Ralph well because our mission had been helping him for well over a year.

But on this particular evening, the roles were reversed and I was in need. The only thing I had eaten that day was a donut from the local Salvation Army, and I was hungry. Ralph had a brown paper lunch bag; he reached in and pulled out a sandwich. "You want half my sandwich, James?"

Let's just stop for a moment. What would you do if a young homeless guy offered you half of his sandwich?

"No, Ralph. I'm not going to take your sandwich from you. You see, you're homeless and I'm . . . well, I'm not really homeless. I've got a home I can go to, and I can have food when I want, and anyway, I'm the one who always helps you. Make sense? I'm the minister and you're the ministry."

Okay, I didn't say that, but I'll admit that I thought it. Thankfully, my hunger overrode my egoistic impulses, and I broke bread with Ralph that evening as we sat on the curb together. I realized then how I had been viewing Ralph and the thousands of others we had helped as objects of my good intentions instead of as individual subjects with the capacity to contribute, and even the capacity to attain the same independence and freedom I enjoyed.

That experience, along with many others you'll read in this book, transformed Watered Gardens Ministries. We shifted from a simple but very busy redistribution center to a complex ministry with hundreds of volunteers focused on complex individual lives. We try to help everyone who walks through our doors unleash their full potential and recognize their worth. From our emergency shelter services, to our family homeless center for moms with kids, to our long-term recovery and work-ready program for men, we've trained ourselves to look beyond the brokenness of people in poverty to focus on the value that each individual can bring to the table. That value is expressed mostly in work. Our Worth Shop, for example, provides the opportunity for everyone to earn what they need.

As we made this monumental shift from a handout ministry to one that challenges clients, we experienced a mass exodus. About two-thirds of the people we used to see every year, twenty-eight hundred in total, dropped out of sight. Where did they go? That question and its answer caused us to launch a campaign to educate our community about the truth of a one-hundred-year-old adage that's been long forgotten: Intelligent giving and intelligent withholding are alike true charity. This campaign grew into the True Charity Initiative. As a result, this initiative now works with organizations nationally to equip community leaders with tools and training that transform the way charity is delivered.

Together, we can effectively fight poverty with authentic, accurate, and actualized charity.

In fact, it is the lack of thoughtfulness in our charity and our unwillingness to withhold that has trapped millions in poverty today, giving rise to a new epidemic of dependency. Unfortunately, our compassion is complicit. It often leads to charitable transactions that offer short-lived satisfaction but fail to deliver people from life-long poverty.

I've seen it firsthand. And through the personal stories, examples, and research in this book, you will be able to experience it alongside me.

In chapter one, we will journey toward justice with the fuel of compassion and the vehicle of charity, elaborating on how compassion and charity can be partners in crimes of injustice. Next, we will unpack the connection between independence and freedom in chapter two, homing in on two specific types of freedom and why they are important to us all. That conversation will naturally lead us to chapter three, where we will dive into the concepts of power and empowerment; here we will also dig into the reality that aid is not the answer to poverty, especially when the government's overreaching attempts to help the poor actually hold them back from experiencing freedom. In chapter four, we will discover how bad charity crowds out good charity, infringing on opportunity and personal liberty; essentially, you don't give what you don't have, and you don't give to a need that has already been met. The same concepts apply to relationships, as we will discuss in chapter five.

Midway through the book is a parable. This story acts as the intermission between the information-heavy part one and the action-oriented application of part two.

In chapter six, we define the reality that there are no shortcuts to charity. Ultimately freedom is valuable, and loving others is a choice, no matter where our journey takes us. Chapter seven is directed toward the practitioner—you and I—or anyone who fills the role of the Good Samaritan. If we want to unleash the full potential of our desire and capacity to help others, we have to recognize our obligation to authentic, accurate, and actualized charity. And for those of us who are philanthropists, chapter eight provides four questions to ask a nonprofit leader before you pledge your financial support.

Finally, chapter nine discusses how effective policy involves everyone, not just elected leaders because all of us have a role to play in policy, from voting for representatives to voicing our opinions and researching current information.

By the end of this book, I hope you discover that compassion has the potential to destroy poverty, but when misguided, it can destroy people. In the same vein, charity can either set people free from poverty or keep them dependent for life.

We must demand of charities, elected officials, and ourselves that we no longer view someone like Ralph as a poor person who has nothing to give, but rather as a unique individual with immense potential who has much to give and everything to gain.

CHAPTER 1

Charity and Justice

JUSTICE

As I pen these words, a fifty-nine-year-old Mexican American man is sitting in a chair in my kitchen with a towel around his neck. My wife makes her way around him in tight semicircles with a variety of haircutting tools. She's on a mission to prepare him for his interview in a few days.

Earlier this evening, I went through some common interview questions over dinner. *What are your strengths? What are your weaknesses?* John's brow creased as he considered them. "Well, I work good with people. Yeah, I can serve, but I'm not very good with mechanical things." I smiled, thinking back to our fishing trip earlier in the day when we had struggled to steer our canoe.

Then, in a sudden burst of confidence, John interrupted my thought: "I think I'm going to get this job. They know I'm just trying to get my life back on track."

Six months ago, his life was not on track. John might even use the term "derailed." Those who knew him saw a homeless man with a chronic drug addiction. They wouldn't expect to see the clear-eyed, clear-minded, and clean-cut man sitting in front of me now. Six months ago, anyone who saw John knew that things weren't right. Tonight, as a student halfway through our mission's long-term character development and work-ready program, John's life is back on track as it ought to be.

Some would call that justice.

What is justice? It depends on what type we're talking about. Distributive justice? Restorative justice? Retributive justice? And how do these varying types of justice fit into the idea of social justice? In 1976 famed economist Friedrich Hayek opened his lecture, "To discover the meaning of what is called 'social justice' has been one of my chief pre-occupations for more than 10 years. I have failed in this endeavor." He concluded that the phrase social justice has "no meaning whatever."[1]

Thinkers like Hayek challenge us to ask if poverty itself is an injustice. Careful consideration reveals the answer is no. Not every ingredient of poverty is an injustice. Factors such as physical debility, accidents, and aptitude may be causative agents; yet they are clearly not injustices. Conversely, parental neglect, abuse, prejudice, exploitation, other violations or transgressions—and even well-intentioned charity that creates dependency—are injustices that create much of the poverty we see today. Some of these injustices played a role in John's downward spiral.

One author simplified it like this: "Truth corresponds to what is; justice to what ought to be."[2] John believes that his sobriety, newfound family, and a job "ought to be." In this book, we'll adopt this simple definition of justice with one caveat: a state of justice or "what ought to be" is not simply an amelioration of poverty's effect, but a clear redress of specific injustices that cause or perpetuate poverty.

Understanding justice as what "ought to be" also requires an elevated anthropology—a belief that each person has innate value, natural rights, a spiritual identity, and a uniqueness that forms the foundation for what ought to be. We are more than animals responding to natural pressures. If that was all we were, there would be no room for this definition of justice. What meaning has "ought to be" if life and death are wrapped up in random events or natural selection by fitness alone? In such a state, there is no "ought to be"; instead, justice is relegated to "whatever happens."

John had subscribed to "whatever happens" for many years and found himself wishing he could cancel his subscription! Then he discovered something radically different from what he had always known. Now, he has traded in a life of deals in darkened alleys for one full of love and truth—a life he believes "ought to be."

Whether you believe John's transformation represents what ought to be happening for the poor and homeless in our nation today, few would disagree that it would certainly be good for our nation.

Wisdom then demands we ask, "How does justice happen?" How did it happen for John? How does this apparent transformation occur? Getting the right answer to that question is vital. And, as you'll find out soon, missing the answer leads us down a road in which charity is loose, liberty is trampled, and John is never free.

COMPASSION

In front of our mission in downtown Joplin, Missouri, there are a few Bradford pear trees in the parkway that cast a bit of shade. If you pass by, you might notice a person leaning up against one or someone reclined under one, exhausted from the mess of life.

One morning, I went to the mission early. The sun was just coming up, and I wandered over to one of those trees and stood there looking at the ground. It must have seemed strange to the homeless man nearby because he approached and asked if I was okay. I said, "I'm just trying to figure out how this happened." He then looked at the base of the tree. There were about fifty cigarette butts all located in a small mound. As I leaned in a bit closer, I could read the label on the butts. Pall Mall.

How did this happen?

"Do you think someone dumped an ashtray?" I asked.

My investigator companion just smiled. "No," he said. "I think someone was just sitting here for a while. That's how that happened."

I shook my head and headed inside the mission. I sat in one of our offices with a large glass window that faced the street. The windows technically aren't made of one-way glass, but they often appear to be. People don't see you, but you can see them using the reflection to check their profiles for anything—hair, clothes—that needs adjusting. Through that window, I saw homeless people caring about how they're perceived, just like you and me.

Usually I'm working, but that morning, I think a part of me simply wanted to understand a bit more about the people I'm serving. More than half an hour went by with me parked in front of that window, watching and listening and praying without anyone knowing I was there.

Young men pretended to be kung fu artists. One young woman without any teeth paraded up and down the sidewalk with obvious hopes of catching attention. One man who'd been beaten up recently, his face still black and blue, just sat on the steps and smoked. Another man solemnly stood on the corner apart from the congregation of a dozen others, staring eastward, the sun lighting his face and the tattoos that covered his arms.

Then I felt compelled to do more than just sit there inside and observe. Suddenly, I really wanted to be *with* them.

And so I stepped out the front door and sat down with about five others on the front steps facing Kentucky Avenue. One lady hit her vape once in a while. A couple of steps down, a young man with an obvious learning disability smoked the real things. To my far left was an elderly lady who also lit up. I was surrounded by smoke. I don't like the smell of it, but that morning, I was glad to be there.

I wasn't there to teach, lead, give, or do. I was just there to be.

Soon, one by one, people began to exit down Artistic Alley toward the library or southward on Kentucky Avenue toward the Salvation Army for donuts and coffee.

Except for Betty.

This short, older woman with white hair, glasses, and worn tennis shoes was the only one who remained on the steps with me (though she wasn't *with* me so much as she was just sitting on the steps smoking). I hadn't spoken to Betty much. I'd seen her in the mission from time to time, but she always seemed a bit crass and unapproachable.

I don't remember which of us began the conversation, but within a few minutes, she was really opening up. She told me about her hopes of having a home again. She told me that her husband died in April of that year, and she had to give up their home. She told me that she lived with her son for a while. And then she told me why she was homeless—because he didn't want her there anymore. Tears began to stream down her face, which looked twenty years older than she was.

I scooted over to sit beside her, and I put my hand on her shoulder. The cigarette smoke might as well have been my own. She was almost finished with her cigarette when she pulled another one from her box, lighting the new one with the old one before she dumped the snub in a tin can beside her.

They were Pall Malls.

Tears still streaming, she then said some very powerful words I'll never forget: "My whole life has never been what I wanted." She leaned into me, putting her head on my chest, and I just held Betty as we both wept and (kind of) smoked that Pall Mall together. And then she lamented those words that had been the theme of my morning but the substance of her life: "*How did this happen?*"

I want you to join me in Betty's story, to sit on those steps with me and embrace a widow who feels lost and lonely.

What I felt then may be what you feel now: Compassion.

Think of compassion not as something you do but more as something you feel. Compassion is an emotion. It's not something we muster up or willfully decide to execute for a particular moment. Compassion is an emotional response we experience when we come face-to-face with injustice and feel the sharp contrast with what ought to be. In fact, the Latin compound root, *cum passus*, means "to suffer with." In the New Testament of the Bible, we discover its Greek form, *splangchizomai*, translated literally as "seated in the gut." That's where it hit me that morning with Betty.

Earlier, we asked the question about John's amazing transformation. *How did this happen?* I know the answer because I've heard John's testimony. He'll tell you it started with a college student who approached him on the streets and felt for him what you just felt for Betty: compassion. It may not seem relevant to a book intended to connect charity and liberty, but you'll soon learn that many of the bureaucratic social mechanisms created to relieve poverty sadly short-circuit compassion and threaten liberty. And if compassion is short-circuited, so also is the action it compels.

CHARITY

Consider justice as our destination. It's where you and I believe things ought to be—that place where a person's poverty and oppression have been replaced with relationship and freedom. To reach this destination, fuel is required. That's compassion. Compassion is the fire, the combustible that drives us toward that end goal of justice. However, having a full gas can in your hands and a map that tells you exactly where you need to go doesn't get you there. You need a vehicle! In our schematic, that vehicle is charity.

Perhaps you've heard the opinion that contrasts charity and justice as mutually exclusive, charity being likened to indiscriminate handouts while justice empowers the poor through a more dignified approach. It's unfortunate that charity has been belittled by some to mean aimless aid. If that's your understanding, I encourage you to discard it.

Charity is the outflow of compassion. It is the action that follows the emotion of empathy. While compassion fuels a desire to bear someone's burden, charity actually bears it. It is the vehicle.

However, all acts of charity don't lead us to the destination of justice any more than all three-point shot attempts result in three points. In fact, a great deal of compassion fuels a tremendous amount of charity that fails to resolve issues of poverty. That's why charity gets a bad rap.

Charity can be effective or ineffective. Effective charity is real help that proves itself in measurable outcomes toward the resolution of poverty. On the other hand, simple aid, such as one-way handouts, has never lifted anyone out of poverty.

In February 2010, near the thirty-day mark after the earthquake in Haiti that destroyed more than three hundred thousand buildings and killed more than one hundred thousand people, our plane landed in Santo Domingo, Dominican Republic. The Port-au-Prince airport in Haiti was still closed due to this natural disaster so, after passing through customs, I hopped in an SUV that was waiting to transport me and a group of volunteers across the border to the Haitian community of Fond Parisien. My background as a physical therapist and wound care specialist was about to be tested in the midst of a chaotic situation among masses of wounded people.

After our last checkpoint, I entered one of the most impoverished nations in the world. As far as I could see along one side of the dirt road were a variety of tents, makeshift huts, and lean-to shelters. In front of them, Haitians sold goods or various foods. The other side of the road was bordered by Lake Azuei.

We stopped and I made my way toward the shoreline with an interpreter at my side. A young boy, about ten years old, approached me with his hand out and one English word he spoke clearly enough: "Dolla, dolla, dolla." I certainly felt compassion for this child whose impoverished country had been rocked by a 7.0 magnitude earthquake. Where were his parents? Did he have a home or was he living in one of these rudimentary shelters? Was he hungry?

I don't recall the answers to some of these questions, but I do recall a desire to answer his poverty with a dollar. It would have been easy, inexpensive, and it might have felt good to satisfy his plea. But I asked him a question instead. "Why do you need it?"

You might have guessed his response: "I'm hungry."

I had noticed a few other boys a little older than this one fishing at the lake's edge. "Why don't you fish like these other boys?"

He pulled a fishing line from his pocket and showed me a bare hook. "I have no bait."

I noticed another boy had three fish on what looked like a coat hanger. I approached him with a dollar in hand and told him I'd like to buy his biggest fish. I'll never forget how he looked me up and down, seemingly assessing my capacity before shaking his head and pointing to his smallest fish. I laughed, pleased at his shrewdness, and sealed the deal. I took the small fish back to the boy and made sure he was able to bait his hook. I don't know if he had any luck, but I do know that he was energized at the prospect of fishing like the others.

At first, it seemed like there were only two possible responses: "Leave me alone" or give him a "dolla." No charity or ineffective charity. What I've learned over nearly two decades of charity work is there's usually a third option (if not a fourth, or a fifth), and the level of effectiveness depends on the amount of time spent listening and investigating.

You could certainly accuse me at this point of too quickly diagnosing the gift of a dollar as ineffective charity. Is it bad to give a dollar? Is it wrong to hand cash to the person holding a cardboard sign at the intersection? Is it wrong to give a fish to a kid? The right answer is, "It depends." It depends on your personal knowledge of each situation. What I am sure of is that simple aid and one-way handouts never lift anyone out of poverty; most often, they create dependency.

In *Toxic Charity*, Robert Lupton delineates five steps to dependency: If you give something to someone once, the person will appreciate it. If you give it a second time, he'll develop an anticipation that you might do it a third. If you do it a third time, he'll expect you'll do it a fourth. A fourth time, he'll feel entitled to the transfer. And a fifth time, he'll be dependent on you for it.[3]

Marvin Olasky in *Tragedy of American Compassion* aptly wrote, "Dependency is merely slavery with a smiling mask."[4] The dependency created by compassionate but careless and thoughtless charity doesn't just trap the poor in dependency—it traps the charitable in paternalism also. Consider these five steps to get there: Give something to someone and you'll feel a sense of exhilaration. Again, and you'll feel useful to who you're helping. A third time and you'll feel necessary. A fourth, essential. And a fifth, paternal.

I will continue in that parallelism by adding to Olasky's thought on dependency as mere slavery: Then also, paternalism is merely subjugation with a smiling mask.

5 Steps to Dependency and Paternalism

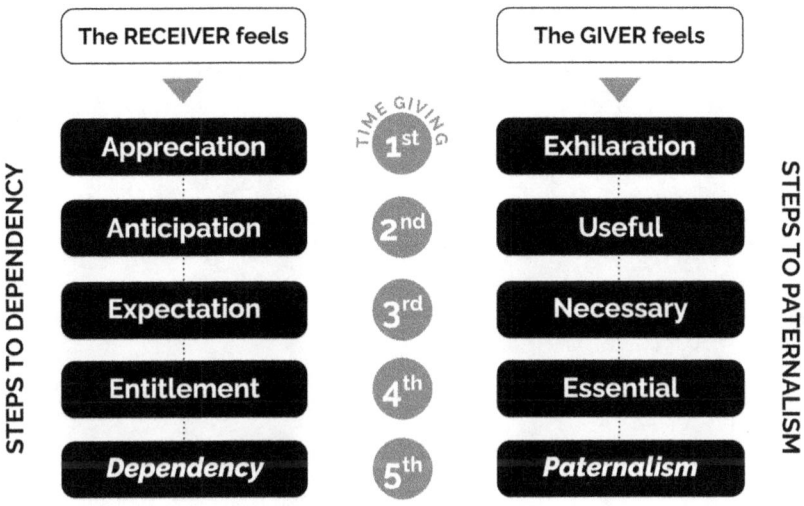

Has our personal charity and national welfare caused this type of unhealthy codependency between those who have and those who have not? In our attempt to close the equity gap, have we inadvertently widened the divide? Are we digressing from a free and prosperous nation known as the land of opportunity to one in which opportunities are being choked out by those who offer dependency instead?

To truly help people trapped in dependent poverty, we must understand how dependence is formed and the strength of its grip on a person. We should also understand its antithesis—independence. In the next chapter, you'll learn more about independence and freedom through the stories of Beth who guards herself from handouts, Kenny who didn't really need them, and Jocelyn who struggled to get free from them.

CHAPTER 2

Independence and Freedom

DEPENDENCY AND BONDAGE

As I walked down the hall of our mission toward our kitchen and food pantry, a lady stopped me. Beth appeared to be in her mid-sixties. I hadn't seen her in the mission before, so we exchanged a few words in the hallway. I learned she had lost her daughter in an accident a few years before and had struggled on a number of fronts, including basic needs like food. She had, in fact, just finished working for a food box and was waiting for it to be prepared by workers in our pantry.

She said, "I know I could have gone somewhere else to get food for free, but I was raised to believe that if I'm able, I should work for what I need." Later, she called and left a message on my office phone: "I just called to say that today, I didn't feel like I was less than anyone else. You made me feel worthy of what I was doing to give back a little . . . treating each other as equals . . . as I feel I was treated today. I just wanted to say thank you."

Homeless or not, our mission provides a way for people to earn their food and meals among other basic needs, and nearly every person who makes it through our doors has the capacity to work in some manner.

More than half of the residents at our mission land gainful employment and the others are able to contribute by helping with recycling, crafts, or other simple tasks. Because almost every person who walks through the doors of our mission has the capacity to earn their food, it has always surprised me that a majority of them have EBT (food stamp) cards. They obviously don't need free food.

The day came when I had to ask. Five members of my team invited five homeless people from our shelter to sit with us and help us understand. It was a relaxed conversation around a large table in our mission's dining hall. From the beginning, the participants were eager to engage in the discussion—our interest in discussing this with them clearly showed them they had something important to share with us. And share they did.

We asked a number of questions: "Do you really need food stamps?" They all agreed they didn't. "Would you be willing to give them up?" They all agreed they wouldn't.

The conversation weaved through a variety of related topics, and I finally asked, "What if we promised you $1,000 in cash after six months if you gave the food stamps up today?"

I remember how silent they were as glances were exchanged. And then, almost simultaneously, they declined.

What?

I was stunned. Each of them was working for daily mission meals. They had already admitted they could get by without food stamps. Yet they declined to entertain the possibility of a payout in six months. Why?

Perhaps it was because six months seems like forever to a person who has thought only three days in advance for most of his life. But when I asked them to explain, one person answered, "If we give them up, we're afraid we won't be able to get back on them again."

Everyone else agreed with the statement, and another person added, "And besides, we don't know how long this place will be around, but food stamps will always be around."

I was sad as we parted that day because I realized there are likely millions of people who feel they could probably get by without government assistance but fear trying. Fearful people are not free people.

WHAT IS FREEDOM?

What does it mean to be a free people? Do you think Beth, who worked for her food, is more free than the food stamp recipient who fears giving up his card?

One day every year, on the Fourth of July, most Americans are given the day off work to celebrate our free nation. We call it Independence Day. What is the connection between independence and freedom? If we consider dependency—like dependence on long-term welfare or continued handouts—to be like bondage, is independence then freedom? And, maybe more importantly, can an independent nation be free if its people are not independent?

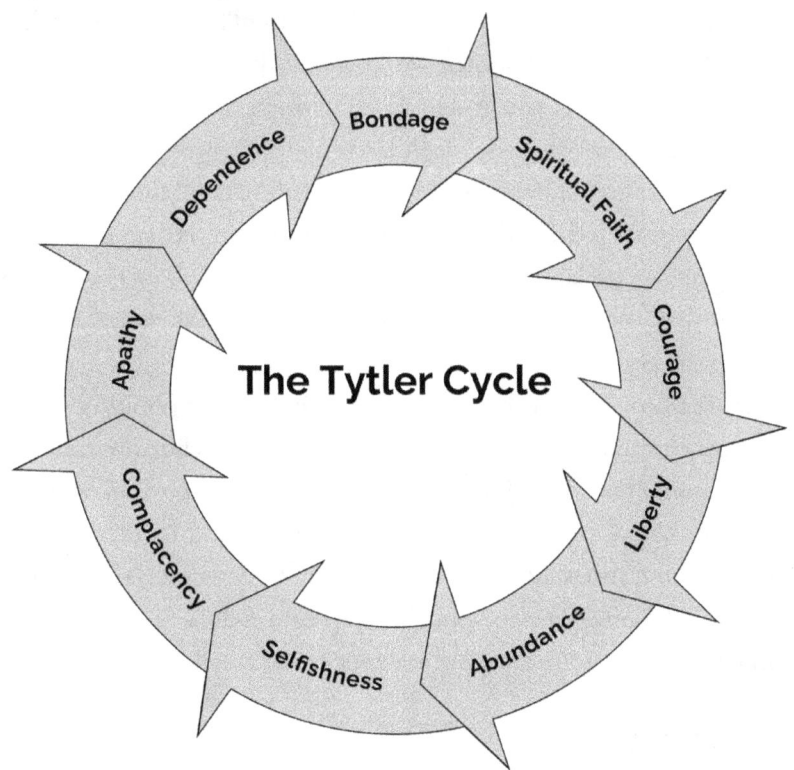

Alexander Tytler, a late eighteenth-century Scottish historian, is often credited for proposing that the rise and fall of nations is cyclical. He posed that nations are born out of bondage because faith empowers a people with courage to rise against forces of oppression. The resulting freedom leads to a people who dream and take risks, creating wealth and abundance. He then points out the great risk of abundance: It tends to stimulate a shift from necessary and purposeful production to selfish consumption and complacency. Complacency progresses to apathy.

And without the drive to produce, dependency is the next step in the cycle, followed by a return to bondage.

Where do you think we are in America? Have we rounded the corner to selfishness or complacency? Is there a generation apathetic to entrepreneurialism and industry? How much of our nation is lost in dependency? Are we truly free?

Does freedom even matter?

It does. Consider freedom as the power or right to act, speak, or think without hindrance or restraint. We can boil that down to two words: unrestricted action. If you and I can act without restriction, then we're free. The freest society is one in which no external force restricts people who in turn restrain themselves from imposing external forces on others.

In our efforts to help those in poverty, much of our welfare public policy represents a lack of self-restraint, placing the federal government in the role of paternal provider that imposes an external, restrictive force on the poor.

Before I explain how that works, know that I'm not pointing a finger at big government programs any more than I am at charities that offer mere material help based on the extent of a person's poverty. Handout charity, public or private, may flow from an admirable intent to help the poor, but it threatens personal freedom, nonetheless. Here's how.

First, let's consider two specific types of freedom. The first is economic freedom, and the second is experiential freedom.

ECONOMIC FREEDOM

Economic freedom is about more than just money. The word "economics," from the compound Greek *oikonomía*, means "management of the house." Economic freedom is the freedom to manage—specifically, to manage one's own resources, including both time and property. This is the type of freedom that most of us think about when we consider freedom.

When there's a crisis, we make economic decisions to manage the situation to the best of our ability with the resources we have at our disposal. When there's a cause we want to support, we may exercise our freedom to manage our schedules or finances by volunteering time or donating money. When facing an intruder, we may choose to manage the situation by fighting back with a weapon or simply taking flight. In other words, economic freedom is the freedom you and I have to manage what is ours for our own best interest (or the interest of others, if we so choose).

Regardless of material poverty, we all have some level of economic freedom. And regardless of wealth, we are all managing under constrained optimization. Put simply, constrained optimization is an economic principle that says no one can do anything and everything he wants—there's always a limit or constraint. That constraint represents a set of boundaries impacting how we manage our resources to optimize our situation. We'll call it our "option space."

We all have "option space," regardless of our poverty or wealth. Kenny, a homeless man and chronic alcoholic, exemplifies this well. Once when he came to our shelter, I came across the twelve-inch by twelve-inch square cardboard sign that he held while standing at stop lights. It was one piece, yet it was folded in such a way that it contained two different two-sided posters. One side could be read or flipped over to express a different message. It could then be opened to read another note and unfolded again to reveal a fourth text.

Kenny had masterfully created four different messages to appeal to different stop-light audiences using one small piece of cardboard. He did a great job optimizing the situation under tight constraints! He was exercising his economic freedom and managing the resource he had for his own best interest in a pretty small option space.

Infringements on economic freedom are external forces that tighten the constraints or shrink the option space. Some cities have passed ordinances to arrest panhandlers. Is that penalty an infringement on Kenny's economic freedom? I'm not in favor of panhandling, but it's hard to not consider an ordinance against it an infringement on freedom. Kenny would certainly argue that it tightens his constraints!

Certainly, our option space is limited by our physical ability, financial capacity, intelligence, or other personal factors. However, as I've already introduced, our option space can also be constrained due to external forces as well. Take the example of an intruder. Most of us would manage that situation to optimize our personal safety and retention of property.

1. Protect yourself and your property with a weapon.
2. Call the police.
3. Flee in a vehicle.

For the sake of our example, consider each of these as a separate option that could define our option space for this situation.

How does that space look if your state's laws restrict you from owning a weapon to protect yourself? Your space just got a little smaller.

What if you discontinue your cell phone service because of increasing corporate taxes that are passed on to you as a consumer? Less space. Maybe you call the police and they tell you that there's a fee in order to have their protection? (Yes, that happens in some countries). Your space just grew even smaller.

Can you come up with other external forces that might restrict your ability to flee in a vehicle? Maybe property taxes prevent you from paying for vehicle registration or gas taxes are high enough that you just haven't been able to drive, and the battery is dead.

Burdensome taxes, restrictive regulations, and government corruption limit our economic freedom and shrink our option space. These forces tighten down the constraints in our example of escaping from an intruder, but imagine the consequences for those trying to escape poverty.

While in Guatemala City in 2018, natives told me a group of aristocrats were in political power. In their desire to hold on to that power, they restricted trade, making it difficult for the poor to access global markets. I saw many items being sold in local markets, but when I suggested to one woman that she could increase revenue by selling on eBay or Amazon, she assured me that taxes make it nearly impossible to ship anything out of the country. If she's correct, this restricted environment certainly represents a tightened constraint on the people of Guatemala. Regulations like this that increase constraint and decrease option space infringe on economic freedom.

How are we, the United States, doing as a nation in the area of economic freedom?

First, consider some of the forces that reduce our option space and constrain our ability to optimize our position. Poorly protected property rights, weak rule of law, government overspending, a heavy tax burden, and restricted trade are some of the ways that our option space has shrunk.

According to the Heritage Foundation's 2022 Index of Economic Freedom, the United States scored 72.1/100.[1] Many Americans believe that our "land of the free and home of the brave" is the freest nation in the world, but we're currently graded with a C and ranked in twenty-fifth place. Why? Well, we scored a C in labor freedom and tax burden, and we're flunking government spending.

For the past several years, we've been sinking further into national debt at the pace of roughly a trillion dollars per year. That's nearly how much the government spends annually to care for the sick, hungry, elderly, and poor. For example, prior to the COVID-19 pandemic, the 2019 national budget projected a $996 billion expenditure in anti-poverty programs, excluding social security and CMS (Medicare), with a deficit of $964 billion.[2]

This highlights the important connection between charity and liberty that we discussed in the previous chapter. We're less free partially because of our national debt, much of which can be attributed to the tremendous spending on anti-poverty programs, a social issue that was once tackled through charity at the local community level.

A free nation is only free if its people are free. National economic freedom cannot be separate from individual economic freedom. Remember that when national debt is high, the value of the dollar is threatened. If the dollar in your pocket isn't worth what it was yesterday, then your option space just grew smaller. And due to our national debt, policymakers will tend to avoid tax reductions (and possibly implement tax increases). More taxes shrink the individual's option space, equating to less freedom.

Is my economic freedom in the United States that different from the shopkeeper in Guatemala? How large (or small) is my option space? Does public assistance strengthen our society or weaken it with infringements?

This is why it is important to advocate for private charity over public assistance. Our current nationalized charity system, however well-intentioned, has grown and grown to the point where it drains all citizens—both those who contribute to the system and those who partake—of wealth and liberty. In trying to provide for those who are struggling and need help, it limits everyone's economic freedom instead.

EXPERIENTIAL FREEDOM

Imagine losing your sense of sight. What if you required assistance to navigate your school, find food in the kitchen, or even use the bathroom? I experienced that when I was in graduate school for physical therapy. We were blindfolded for the day to gain personal insight into the challenges of being blind. Thankfully, I was assigned a partner who guided me well through that day, and I managed it without any injuries. But I certainly learned that mobility and communication are restricted in a dark world. You can bet that when I took off that blindfold at the end of the day, I felt liberated!

Obviously, the ability to visually experience the world around me enhanced my freedom and unrestricted action.

In general, the ability to experience life to its fullest advances freedom. I even believe that experiential freedom is a prerequisite to economic freedom.

Jocelyn was addicted to drugs for more than two decades and was, at one point in her life, relegated to taking shelter in a cardboard box on Skid Row in Los Angeles. When she was assigned more than four hundred community service hours at our mission because of her legal troubles, we got to know each other. She found freedom from her drug addiction and came to faith in Christ. For the first time in her adult life, she was clean. She enrolled in a junior college and then went on to study social work and counseling at a university.

From anyone's perspective, Jocelyn appeared to be a success story. Yet in her own words, she was still addicted: She feared giving up her food stamps.

After much reassurance from her new community, she made the leap and gave me her food stamp card. Shortly after that, a local news station learned that we were challenging people to give up welfare, and they wanted to do a story. When they interviewed Jocelyn, she said, "It was harder for me to get free from food stamps than it was for me to get free from heroin." Before that, Jocelyn may have been clean, but she wasn't free.

As she progressed, she admitted a fresh fear of working, of making too much money, because it would result in the loss of benefits.

Welfare is the rope that has tethered millions of Americans to the government. Too many people who are dependent on welfare have lost sight of the constraints those benefits have put on their own capacity and potential. How can anyone measure his option space if he can't press the limits of his ability?

Before giving up her EBT card, Jocelyn had never had the confidence that she could feed herself or realize her full earning potential in her work because she had been tethered to the state for most of her life. To her, the thought of cutting the rope felt impossible. But in reality, her boundaries—the fullest extent of her abilities to provide for herself through her work—were actually far beyond the length of that welfare rope. There was a fence that she knew nothing about, a defined space limited only by her capacity. And that distance was much greater than the short rope that strung her to the state.

Experiential freedom is the freedom to explore those boundaries. It may seem like an abstract tether of fear should hardly be counted as an infringement on liberty, but consider the grown elephant. It can be held in place by a weak rope tethered to a peg in the ground. Nothing holds it back except for the fact he's been conditioned since birth by a trainer. The trainer binds the baby elephant with a rope and, failing to ever experience freedom from it, he becomes conditioned to his bondage, growing into a twelve-thousand-pound adult who believes he can't break loose. Is he free?

When Jocelyn believed she couldn't escape dependency on the state, was she free?

This type of conditioning is conveyed well in Martin Seligman's famous 1967 "learned helplessness" study in which he confined dogs into different groups. Dogs in the treatment group were yoked in pairs and shared a metal shock plate floor, each with a depressible panel. When a shock was applied to the floor, one of the panels could turn it off while the other did nothing. The dogs with "working" panels (group one) learned how to turn the shock off. The panels for the other dogs (group two), however, did nothing, and so they could not perform an action to terminate a random intermittent jolt. The shock was actually being turned off by the dog beside them with a working panel.

The dogs were then moved to shuttle boxes with an easy exit made available to escape a shock. Group one took advantage and escaped. Sadly, the dogs in group two learned their effort in the first scenario did nothing, so they made no attempt to escape the shock in the second scenario. They had learned helplessness.

After this groundbreaking study, Seligman and other researchers went on to prove that the phenomenon of learned helplessness occurs in people, too.[3] Just as the subjects in the original study believed effort was not the key to escape pain, our system of welfare and charity has conditioned millions of people to believe their effort is not the key to escape poverty.

What's worse is that conditioning—this susceptibility to believe effort will yield no results—is not just reinforced by our current welfare system. I have seen many cases over the last two decades where the current welfare system actually *threatens* effort through negative feedback.

Behavioral psychologists call that punishment.

Randy was struggling. He had a heart to serve at the mission, and I wanted to see him succeed. One day, he came into my office and shared that he had an interview for a part-time job. I joined him in his excitement and asked him to share more details. He said, "I can only work part-time because a full-time job will hurt my benefits." Like Jocelyn, Randy feared that the more he worked, the worse things would be. If learned helplessness paralyzes someone from trying, the threat of punishment will paralyze them even more. I can't count the number of times I have seen this detrimental disincentive at work.

It is an affront to experiential freedom, the unrestricted experience of natural cause-and-effect relationships in life.

A frustrated grade school principal shared that her students had each been given a backpack full of supplies and treats to begin the year, and they were leaving these goods strewn about the hallways, classrooms, and lockers. "They just don't seem to care about the work that went into this," she lamented. That's because it wasn't *their* work that went into it.

This type of charity has short-circuited the natural cause-and-effect relationship of time and value. When we spend our time working for something, we tend to value it more. This leads to the next natural cause and effect of loss and pain. When we lose something we've worked for, we feel it. These students didn't value their backpacks full of supplies, and they didn't feel pain from losing them either.

How does a disruption of these cause-and-effect relationships represent an infringement on one's liberty? When we don't associate value with the things we possess or fail to feel pain at their loss, then we haven't grasped the important cause-and-effect relationship of work and gain. Typically, the harder you work, the more you gain.

The failure to experience this natural effect will always result in learned helplessness. Consider these two ways learned helplessness occurs in humans. Either people are subsidized, reducing the drive to work or people are exploited through unfair compensation. Either way, these injustices teach one lesson: Work doesn't pay off, so don't do it.

When someone doesn't work and is sustained in poverty, he learns helplessness. When someone works but doesn't receive remuneration worth his labor, he quits working.

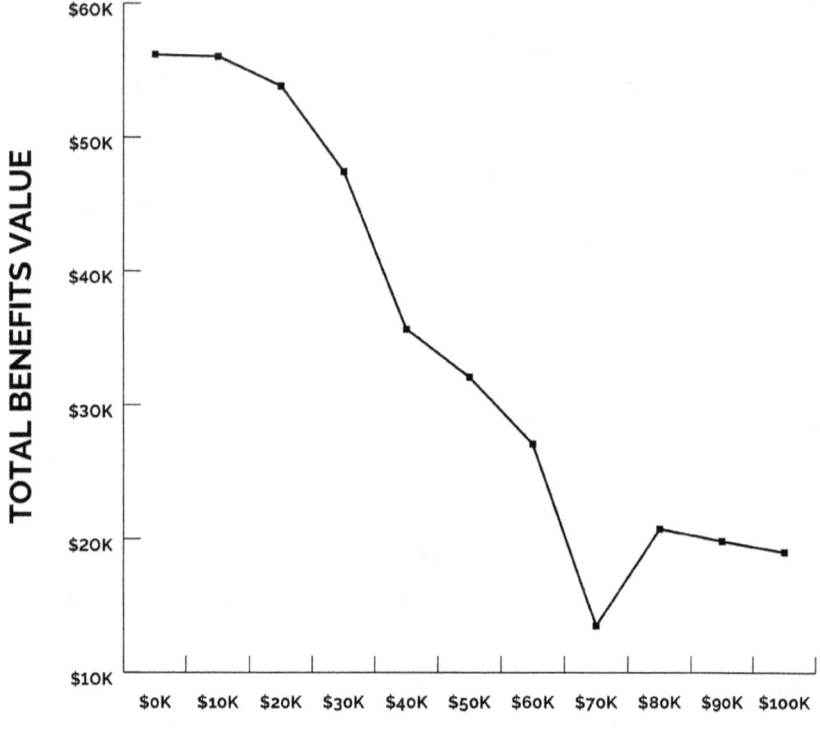

FIGURE 1
SOURCE: Federal Reserve Bank of Atlanta Benefits Cliffs Across the U.S. Powered by Policy Rules Database
(https://emar-data-tools.shinyapps.io/prd_dashboard/)

Thoughtless charity and careless relief contribute to both scenarios. Whether it's handing out cash or dumping goods in developing nations, indiscriminate aid always disconnects the work/gain relationship. Means-tested welfare programs, when a person has qualified for and expects a benefit, pervert the natural work/gain relationship to one of work and pain.

This is what Randy had grown used to. He believed that he qualified for an early SSI disability check. Even with the opportunity and ability

FIGURE 2
SOURCE: Federal Reserve Bank of Atlanta Benefits Cliffs Across the U.S. Powered by Policy Rules Database
(https://emar-data-tools.shinyapps.io/prd_dashboard/)

---

to work full time, Randy declined out of fear that work would result in pain or loss.

Although the fear that work may make things worse is a restriction on freedom, research indicates that when a person breaks through that fear, the "shock" will not be as long or as hard as they expected. Research from the Foundation for Government Accountability reveals that welfare-to-work reform in Arkansas, Florida, Kansas, and Maine has resulted in thousands who went back to work and more than doubled their income.[4]

However, depending on how things are structured in each state, the "benefits cliff" (or welfare cliff) can represent a punishment too severe to consider. For example, in 2023, a single parent with two kids in Greene County, Missouri, who earned $32,000 per year actually qualified for about $40,000 in benefits (fig.1), bringing the annual household income equivalency to just over $70,000, slightly more than the average living expenses (fig.2) for such a family.[5]

Looking closely at figure 2 makes clear the disincentive to advance at work. As soon as the parent in this scenario makes above $32,000 per year, a "cliff" is experienced from a drop in benefits that reduces the overall standard of living. Note that the same standard is not realized again until earned income reaches nearly $58,000 per year.

Having worked with thousands of impoverished people, I'm convinced that the fear of falling off the welfare cliff—the fear of working—is a very real and powerful restraint on those who could achieve much more than what the state could ever supply.

"Greg" is a great, yet tragic, example of this. He was abused by his father, sexually molested by his stepfather, and witnessed a murder in his own home all before he was thirteen years old. It's not hard to understand how he ended up on the streets, homeless and addicted.

When I first met this tall, middle-aged man, I noticed how his long hands trembled due to his drug addiction. He knew he needed help and wanted information about our long-term recovery and work-ready program, Forge. One of the program's expectations turned him away almost immediately: He had to give up all sources of government support. At that time, Greg had what he called a "government package": a government housing voucher, a food stamp card, and early disability benefits. Later, he told me that giving up that package to enter our program was the hardest decision he had ever faced in his life. In his mind, giving it up was tantamount to jumping off a cliff. Today, however, he's a full-time over-the-road truck driver and completely independent of government support.

Greg is free.

Unfortunately, there are millions of Americans who have the same potential to break free from dependency but have never experienced freedom from the tether long enough to know their limits and experience liberty. Yet for freedom's potential to be realized, it requires more than a knowledge of expanded limits. It requires empowerment and effort. In this next chapter, you'll learn how April's effort saved her family, how Carmen's lack of it failed her, and how Charles's effort propelled him from homelessness to small business owner.

CHAPTER 3

Empowerment

THE POWER OF EMPOWERMENT

I first met April in her late twenties. She was addicted to methamphetamine, had lost her children, and her marriage was failing. She was often alone and homeless and had been dependent on state welfare since she was sixteen. After building relationships with us at the mission, she eventually came to faith in Christ, got sober, and started a junior college clerical training program. I remember when she walked into my office toward the end of her education. She was confident and professionally dressed—practically unrecognizable from the shaky homeless girl I had first met months before. In order to complete her clerical training program, she needed to complete an internship, and so she asked if she could intern for the mission. I gladly said yes!

April completed her program, reunited with her family, and saved her marriage. After her internship, we hired her, and she managed our mission's main office for five years. She's not only free from welfare but went on to start a women's recovery ministry where she teaches self-reliance. In a filmed testimony, she shared that "Watered Gardens[1] taught me how to be self-sufficient. They taught me how to take care of myself as opposed to leaning into government assistance."[2]

Anyone who knows April's story would say that she has been empowered. Giving people power is key to helping them escape poverty. Where does it come from? How is it nurtured and protected? And how does our current system of government taxation impact the power of both the taxed and the beneficiary?

THE RIGHT ROLE OF GOVERNMENT

As you've discovered in the first two chapters, I favor a limited federal government, especially when it comes to helping our neighbors in poverty. Although I take a firm stand against legislated redistribution of wealth to fight poverty, I am even more staunchly opposed to the government doing the job *first*, before family, friends, and the local community.

In April 2020, COVID-19 was quickly making its way around the United States. Airports were packed as people raced to get home before travel was restricted, businesses were only serving to-go food, and schools were shutting down. On one of those afternoons, I was on a video call with about twenty other leaders in my city, hoping to develop a plan to reduce an outbreak among the homeless population. The chair of the meeting addressed me. "James, I know you're opposed to government intervention when it comes to helping the poor. Are you able to support a plan that may use government funds?"

With every other leader waiting for my response, I said, "You're right. I am always in favor of neighbor helping neighbor before the state helps your neighbor. With that being said, this is a worldwide pandemic and a national emergency. There's certainly an arguable role for the federal government to support the states in a time like this."

In a true national emergency, the federal government has a role to play in mitigating loss of life. Such intervention, if limited to genuine crises, does nothing to negatively impact empowering the poor.

However, when the government takes from one to alleviate the poverty of another, power is stolen from both, first by taking property and then by redistributing it, which fosters dependency. Power and property are interchangeable and must both be protected for the sake of the poor as well as those who provide the pathway out of poverty.

POWER, RIGHTLY UNDERSTOOD

Which brings us back to April. Remember, she had been empowered, and she made a point to note that her empowerment came because she resisted the urge to rely on government assistance.

What, exactly, does it mean to empower someone? To give someone the power or authority to do something.

Empowerment requires power, and if empowerment is good, then power must also be good. Unfortunately, the word "power" often stirs completely different emotions than the word "empowerment." What do you think of when you hear the word "power"? Inequity? Oppression? Corruption? How about when you hear the word "empower"? Boldness? Courage?

In a now-famous 1887 letter to the Archbishop of the Church of England, Lord Acton wrote, "Power tends to corrupt and absolute power corrupts absolutely." This may be Acton's most well-known line and, at first glance, sheds a negative light on power.

But consider the broader context of this famous line:

> I cannot accept your canon that we are to judge Pope and King unlike other men, with a favourable presumption that they did no wrong ... Power tends to corrupt and absolute power corrupts absolutely. Great men are almost always bad men, even when they exercise influence and not authority ... There is no worse heresy than that the office sanctifies the holder of it. That is the point at which ... the end learns to justify the means.[3]

Acton's letter is not about power so much as it is about human immorality generally. Acton was protesting the idea that people should not be critical of their leaders, whether in religion like the pope or in government like the king. His argument pushed back on the belief that authority alone determines what is moral and decent.

Certainly, as Acton argues, having power doesn't make someone right or good. But does power tend to make someone wrong or bad? Does power always corrupt? I think we need to look a little deeper.

When I was in undergraduate chemistry, we were charged with a lab exercise to create banana oil from a mixture of chemicals. Before long, Bunsen burners were on at every station with beakers full of bubbling fluid. The aroma that filled the room made it easy to imagine that we were standing in the middle of a banana pudding factory.

Oddly, my beaker was the only one completely inactive. I was mystified. I had mixed the chemicals properly. The burner was on high. There was simply no reaction. Then I realized my error: I had forgotten to put in my boiling chip! The boiling chip is a small rock of calcium carbonate that serves as a catalyst for the reaction.

That mistake was dwarfed by my next mistake: I dropped the chip in the heated mixture. Immediately, an explosion of banana oil covered me, my lab partner, and my textbook. For the rest of the semester, every time I opened my chemistry book, the fruity aroma reminded me of that mistake.

What does this have to do with power? Power is like that boiling chip—not dangerous on its own, but only when improperly handled. In fact, power serves as an important catalyst for the reaction of capital and entrepreneurialism to yield poverty's end, the product of wealth creation.

Although it is true that with greater power comes greater risk, power is not inherently the source of the problem. Rather, the problem is greed, envy, and pride that, when mixed with power, corrupts what was originally intended for good.

CORRUPTING POWER

In its simplest form, power has everything to do with work. In fact, in any physics book, you'll find power defined as a function of work (the amount of energy spent to move an object) divided by time. If we adhere to this definition for our context, then power is the ability of a person to move things. And the ability to move more in a shorter period of time is a demonstration of greater power.

People who have power can be considered "movers and shakers." The founder of Amazon, Jeff Bezos, is someone who quite literally moves a lot in a very short amount of time (thank you, Prime two-day shipping). His company shipped 2.3 billion packages in 2019[4] and is poised to surpass FedEx and UPS as the largest delivery service in the US.[5] Shipping more than six million packages every day, few would argue that Jeff Bezos is not a powerful man.

But is he *too* powerful? If you type that question in a search engine, you'll likely find a post by IBM software developer Saul Venskutonis, who answers with a confident "yes."[6] In one post, he points out that Jeff Bezos has half a million employees, more than six hundred thousand followers on his personal Twitter account, spends millions lobbying the government, and collects an inconceivable amount of predictive data to know what his customers will want next. No wonder Venskutonis blogged, "Jeff Bezos certainly has too much power for a single human." But is he right?

Given Bezos's status today, it's easy to think he might have too much power now, but what about in 1995 when he sold books out of his garage using servers that weighed on his house's electrical system so much that his wife couldn't use her hair dryer without blowing a fuse? Every time a book sold, a bell would ring, and he and his small team would dash to the computer to see if they knew the person who had placed the order. In those days of selling books, few would have thought him to be a powerful man.

Did he become too powerful when he netted his first $100,000? Maybe when he paid off his first real warehouse? Did he breach a threshold when he shook the President's hand, or when he earned his first million dollars? We could deliberate for an untold amount of time to determine at which particular point Jeff Bezos might have crossed the line of "too powerful," but I believe we would find it to be very arbitrary and more likely nonexistent. Why? Because power is not the problem. It is simply the force by which things are moved and work is done. The power that Bezos used to launch that business in his garage was good, and though he has more power (and money) today, the quality of a thing is not changed by its quantity. The quality of power is not changed by its measure but by man's intent.

Through effective charity, April was empowered and liberated from addiction, poverty, and government dependency. Like Jeff Bezos, she has gained more power with time. With empowerment, she has done even more good, now leading other women out of poverty. In my opinion, she is what many would call a "mover and a shaker!" Could she use her new power to exploit women by signing them up for welfare and then using the benefits for her own gain? Yes. Would power be to blame? No.

To truly understand the importance of empowerment in regard to liberty and charity, we need to look more closely at power's original condition.

POWER AND WORK

Power is a part of the original blueprint for the universe—not just in God, or in creation, but in humanity. In the opening chapters of the first book of the Bible, we read that the first humans were empowered by God in some specific ways. They were given both mind and body in order for them to be good stewards of creation. With that stewardship, and the command to "tend" or "keep" the garden, they were given authority over property and opportunity through work. Thus, work, authority, opportunity, and power all existed in the original condition of perfection and unspoiled freedom. For Adam and Eve, these were the building blocks for society by which humanity would go on to create wealth and establish prosperous cities.

How did that happen? How did the earliest humans move from being naked and nomadic to being prosperous and stable? The answer to that question is the answer to poverty, and it has everything to do with power and work.

With the mind and body that humanity was endowed with at creation, they planted, harvested, hunted, harnessed, fashioned, crafted, built, and beautified. Reflecting the image of their Creator and the ultimate Producer, they used their own power and capitalized like crazy.

Now, "capitalize" and "capitalism" are words that make some cringe and others delight, but regardless of how we react, humans are natural capitalists in the technical sense. We'll look more into this important truth later, but for now, simply consider this: People sow with the seeds they've harvested, hunt with the weapons they've fashioned, build with the tools they've crafted, and then, with what they've profited, turn around and repeat it all. This process not only amplifies their gains, but all the while beautifies the world around them with what they've created. This is how humanity left mere survival and subsistence behind and created art, music, and culture.

From the days of wandering in the woods to now, a tremendous amount of wealth has been created. Today, the same combination of mind, body, and stewardship are still used every day by people in free societies all over the world to create value and lift themselves out of poverty. For the most part, they do it under their own power by the work of their own hands. Ideally, they will receive encouragement and support from those around them, but ultimately, if a person doesn't lift himself out of poverty, he will remain in it. No one is "lifted" out of poverty by the effort of other people alone.

Whenever assistance or aid is rendered in the name of charity but does not allow the recipient to capitalize on their own mind, body, and stewardship, it becomes nothing less than a cradle of support rendering them dependent and powerless. This is a failed outcome of charity because no one who is powerless is also free.

My experience as a physical therapist has given me two key insights into why this relationship between power and freedom is true. First, I'm reminded of a patient from years ago diagnosed with Guillain-Barré syndrome, a rare autoimmune disorder in which the peripheral nervous system is attacked leading to paralysis. In my patient's case, it was complete paralysis. At the peak of his symptoms, he couldn't move, speak, or even breathe on his own.

Amazingly, this rare condition often reverses over time, and thankfully, it did for my patient, too. He made a full recovery, learning to breathe, talk, and walk on his own again. At the height of his disease process, this man's condition was the epitome of powerlessness. Although he couldn't have responded, had I dared to lean over the hospital bed and his paralyzed body to ask it, I'm sure his full-functioning mental faculty would have been appalled at the question, "How free do you feel right now?"

I imagine he would have thought something like this: "How free do I feel? I can't do anything on my own! I'm completely dependent on the work of the nurse, the work of my wife, the work of this machine I'm stuck on. I have no power to do anything on my own, even to direct my own course of care. How free am I? I'm powerless!"

At an event years later, I saw that man again. As he greeted me and reminded me of our history, I immediately recalled moments of this man struggling to walk in parallel bars and then progressing to stairs. He worked hard, got stronger, and eventually regained his ability to walk. Although he was thankful for my help, I'm sure if I asked him who was responsible for lifting him out of his hospital bed and restoring his freedom of movement, he would have responded, "Me." It was him. It certainly wasn't the ventilator. That may have kept him alive, but it never set him free.

This extreme case can help us understand the proper relationship between one's own power and personal freedom. We're often guilty of overlooking it. Either through welfare or ineffective aid, we hand out provisions that might be keeping people alive, but they never set them free.

For this reason, Rwandan pastor John Rucyahana passionately opposes western aid sent to his nation. In an interview, he powerfully said, "Instead of training job seekers, we train job makers. We need to be able to move from aid to production."[7]

Most experts agree that aid alone is not the answer to poverty. Simply put, charity that empowers people to escape the bonds of poverty requires work. In order to embrace a view of charity based on work, we have to deal with the conundrum that though work is right, it rarely feels good.

CHALLENGE DEVELOPS

My second insight came shortly after I began practicing physical therapy. I stepped into a patient's hospital room and a family member said, "Oh, it's the physical terrorist." I laughed, but I don't think my patient thought it too funny. I'm sure its genesis had much to do with the pain a patient incurs with physical rehabilitation—pain most often inflicted by the therapist. That wasn't the last time I heard that nickname.

The family member who first tagged me a "terrorist" may have wished for me to gently scoop his family member up in my arms and carefully move her from her hospital bed to a comfortable bedside chair rather than challenging her to do it herself. More so, my patient probably wished for that! However, every physical therapist knows this two-word sentence to be true: Challenge develops. A therapist who fails to implement challenges is one who fails to empower his patient. A patient who does not experience challenges does not develop strength and mobility. Without building strength and regaining mobility, the patient remains bound to a bed of infirmity until he perishes.

So it is with charity. If help for the impoverished person fails to provide challenges to help him overcome through his own work, then he remains bound to a bed of poverty until he perishes. Such a comparison may seem a bit philosophical, but the truth is that too often our current social welfare system and well-intentioned aid are literally trapping people in poverty until they die.

A Pew Charitable Trust study revealed that 70 percent of those born into poverty will die in poverty. At the time of this writing, poverty rate in the United States is 13 percent, and only 4 percent of poor families receive no welfare, which means that about twenty-six million people are on a path to die in poverty, having never found freedom from dependency.[8]

If our charity is to help the poor rise from such a fate, then work is required. Our ability to work and overcome challenges is the very reason why humanity was empowered with both mind and body.

Work is necessary for us to be fully free in this world, and therefore truly human. While work is essential, it is not all that's required for a society to be both charitable and free. Property is as well.

POWER AND PROPERTY

The primary way an individual can rise from his supine position of poverty is through his own power and work. However, to simply stand is far from the freedom he's able to achieve. It would be good to run and leave poverty far behind! But that kind of freedom requires the power and freedom to build.

There's an old milk barn on my property with a barn swallow nest. When I walk in the barn in the spring, the bird fearfully barrels up through the rafters to escape my threat. I certainly have the ability, and probably the right, to remove the nest, but I've left it undisturbed for four years. It may seem strange to leave it, but then again, I didn't build it.

I asked my two-year-old grandson, "Whose nest is this?"

He responded as you might think: "The bird's."

But is it really? A bird's nest is often made of a combination of straw, grass, fur, hair, leaves, moss, wool, mud, or twigs. Some of that may have come from my property, my dog, or even my wife's long hair! And yet no one in his right mind would look at a bird's nest and assert that it belongs to the dog, the farmer, or his wife. We would all establish that the nest is the bird's because he built it. It's the beaver's dam because the beaver built it. It's the spider's web because . . . well, you get the point. When a creator labors to build something, it becomes the creator's property.

Does this property have value? Many thoughtful people would say so. The spider is made fat by catching food in its web, the beaver's home is safe by its dam, and the bird's family grows in its nest. Provision. Safety. Growth. Taken together, it sounds like a cure for poverty. How? Power was converted to labor and labor converted to property. This is how it works in a free society when property rights are protected.

What do you think my grandson's response would be if we watched a hawk attack that barn swallow in the milk barn until it drove off the mama bird, only to grasp the nest in its claws and fly away with it? He doesn't know the word "injustice" yet, but I'm sure he would sense it. Most likely you would, too. Why? Because a creature with more power took the property of what the weaker one had labored to build. The result? Homeless birds and baby chicks without a future.

Shouldn't humans do better? For the poor to be free of poverty, protection of property is vital and necessary. If a man uses his power to build something and then it is taken from him, is he not moved toward poverty? And if it is taken from those who have and given to those who don't, is it not doubly unjust by stripping the former of his property and the latter of his drive to build?

This is why redistributionism is an antagonist to empowerment; it moves one closer to poverty and perversely incentivizes the other to stay there.

French political philosopher Alexis de Tocqueville saw that perverse incentive at work as he explored England's impoverished landscape in the mid-1800s. England's sweeping welfare legislation left many of the poor with no impetus to work. Those who subsisted on the alms of the state were termed paupers by Tocqueville:

> There are, however, two incentives to work: the need to live and the desire to improve the conditions of life. Experience has proven that the majority of men can be sufficiently motivated to work only by the first of these incentives. The second is only effective with a small minority. Well, a charitable institution indiscriminately open to all those in need, or a law which gives all the poor a right to public aid, whatever the origin of their poverty, weakens or destroys the first stimulant . . .[9]

This truth is not exclusive to Europe in the 1800s. I see it regularly on the streets of my city.

I was leaving the mission one afternoon as a young woman named Carmen bounded down the sidewalk exuberantly shouting, "I got an apartment! I got an apartment!" She had been a resident in our shelter due to homelessness. As she rushed to where I stood, I thought she was going to wrap me up in a celebratory hug. "That's exciting," I agreed.

Knowing that it was federally funded housing and that she wasn't employed, I followed, "You better get a job so you can keep that apartment."

Carmen threw out her arms and cheerfully replied, "I don't have to. I got disability, too!"

However, neither the Department for Housing and Urban Development (HUD) nor the Social Security Administration (SSA) knew Carmen. We did. She had been earning her shelter, meals, and clothing by working in our mission's Worth Shop and it became obvious to us she had the ability to provide for herself if encouraged and challenged to do so. Unfortunately, because so many federally funded programs have goals to help homeless people file for SSDI (Social Security Disability Insurance) or SSI (Supplemental Security Income), the homeless are increasingly being steered toward public aid rather than toward a path of self-reliance.

The goal of SSI/SSDI Outreach, Access, and Recovery (SOAR) is to increase access to SSI/SSDI for eligible adults who are experiencing or at risk of homelessness and have a serious mental illness, medical impairment, and/or a co-occurring substance use disorder.[10]

A mental health outreach program provides free urinary analyses for homeless and poor people trying to get back into the workforce. Before the drug test is administered, a preliminary screening question is asked: "Have you ever suffered any emotional trauma?" One homeless man, Mark, answered, "Yes" and was diverted to an appointment with a psychiatrist who diagnosed him. He was then assisted by the staff to apply for SSDI. When Mark told me this, he said, "I just went in to get a drug test so I could go to work!"

Certainly, there are people struggling with chronic homelessness who have true and severe mental health or physical disabilities, which are a barrier to gainful employment. However, the average annual number of early disability awards among the working age has doubled in the last decade.[11] This clearly shows that many others like Mark and Carmen are being diverted from work—from building their own nests— to subsisting on others.

Even if I told my grandson that the hawk took the swallow's nest so he could help some disabled birds in the neighboring row of woods, I doubt he would have conceived it as charity.

Although we have already discussed how tax earnings are diverted to government programs, the purpose of this chapter is to illuminate the importance of an individual's power as the core to his empowerment and its inseparability from work. In particular, the importance of this section is to grasp the value of building property to broaden freedom from poverty. If a man's nest can't be protected from an aggressor, he does not have a solid foundation to build a more secure future.

One may contend that taxing a rich person for poverty relief programs won't damage his nest. Yet the answer to that argument is fickle. What kind of justice frowns on the hawk when he takes from the swallow but smiles when he takes from the eagle?

My comparison of the state to an aggressive hawk may seem like a stretch, but consider our nation's own Declaration of Independence and how every person, whether strong, weak, rich, or poor, is created with specific and unalienable rights: Life, Liberty and the pursuit of Happiness. This line reveals that the authors of that Declaration were certainly influenced by and likely recounting John Locke's *Two Treatises of Civil Government*:

> The state of nature has a law of nature to govern it, which obliges every one: and reason, which is that law, teaches all mankind, who will but consult it, that being all equal and independent, no one ought to harm another in his life, health, liberty, or possessions.[12]

Was it right for our Founding Fathers to translate Locke's argument for the rightful protection of possessions or property to the personal pursuit of happiness? To answer this question, let's focus less on the word "happiness" and more on the word "pursuit." What's required to pursue anything? Liberty. And when you pursue something, does it not also deliver some degree of happiness? Our Founding Fathers believed that a government's infringement on this pursuit was a grievous act against a man's natural rights. What was their exhortation to a people when under such constraint?

> "... whenever any Form of Government becomes destructive of these ends, it is the Right of the People to alter or to abolish it, and to institute new Government, ..."

And if the trespasses continue, reducing the people under despotism,

> "... it is their right, it is their duty, to throw off such Government, and to provide new Guards for their future security."

In other words, kill the hawk.

Place your vote. Speak up in the public square. Support local charity and work instead of government welfare programs. Education or affluence is not required to understand that state-funded charity is a trespass against another's liberty.

Not long ago during a class, I drew a diagram of two stick figures on a chalkboard. "If this person has money and decides to give it to this other one, what's this called?"

The students of our long-term program, primarily recovered addicts and ex-criminals, got it right: "Charity."

I drew a third stick figure. "Let's call this person the government. If he takes it from this person and gives it to the other, what's that called?"

I expected to hear, "Welfare," but one student, Keith, immediately blurted out, "That's a felony!" Keith, who has a strong experiential understanding of criminality, then pointed at the recipient stick figure and said, "... and he's an accomplice!"

We all laughed at Keith's quick wit that day, and maybe no one in the room but me realized how much his fun matched the sentiment of early nineteenth-century French economist, Frédéric Bastiat. Had Bastiat been in class with us that day, he may have stood to cheer Keith's insight. In *The Law*, Bastiat identifies this state-coerced transfer of one's property to another as legal plunder:

> But how is this legal plunder to be identified? Quite simply. See if the law takes from some persons what belongs to them, and

gives it to other persons to whom it does not belong. See if the law benefits one citizen at the expense of another by doing what the citizen himself cannot do without committing a crime.[13]

After a discussion about this kind of legal plunder, I've had people give me their food stamp cards. "I don't really need it," is what one man said as he handed me his welfare card. "I never knew it was taking something from someone else."

If someone is free and uses his freedom to translate his time into property through the vehicle of work, then when any institution takes that property and gives it to another, it is taking the very time he has spent earning it. And if freedom is spending your time how you choose, then taking someone's property is also stripping that individual of freedom. This simple yet powerful illustration has resulted in scores of people turning over their welfare cards. Those cards are now pinned on a wall in our mission with a placard above it applauding those who took a virtuous step to support liberty. More importantly, turning in those cards contributed to *personal* liberty. You read about the success stories of John in chapter one, Jocelyn in chapter two, and April at the beginning of this chapter. Part of their journey to freedom from poverty included voluntarily turning in their food stamp cards and relying on compassionate, private charity instead.

Those are anecdotes, but research also bears this out. In my state of Missouri, when work requirements for food stamps were enforced in 2016, more than 85 percent of able-bodied adults dropped off the welfare roll, and their incomes more than doubled through more work and new jobs.[14] Whether they are incentivized or inspired, when people choose to walk away from welfare, they go to work and convert their own power into property. And just as power can be converted to property through work, property can be converted to power.

Understanding this can result in a spiral upward from poverty. This process is the simplest form of capitalism and how wealth is created.

Charles is a good example and another one of those brave souls who gave up his food stamps for something better. When he first came to our mission, he was penniless, homeless, and addicted to drugs. We gave him a place to rest his head and eat hot meals. It wasn't much but, coupled with encouragement and accountability, he capitalized on the little we gave him and developed strength in his body and sobriety of mind. He was, to a very small extent, empowered. He then used his new health to enroll in our long-term men's program. He continued to gain more strength, knowledge, and confidence. He then began operating our mission's lawn care social enterprise, earning his own paycheck for the first time in decades. He took those earnings and rented his own apartment. He's now been employed at the mission for five years, has his own pickup truck, and just closed on the purchase of his own home. And that lawn care business? The mission no longer owns it. He does. It's easy to see how Charles used his property to empower himself to gain more property. He's been spiraling upward since we've known him.

You might think that this process could have been jump-started by public welfare rather than private charity, but one statement in Charles's testimony debunks the idea: "I came to Watered Gardens one night and I was accepted. They loved me and became my family. They fed me and gave me a place to rest my head."

That's the beauty of charity! Charity not only loves him for who he is, but it loves him enough to put him to work to earn his bed and meals. That's the kind of charity that empowers someone to freedom.

By creating wealth for himself, Charles has expanded his option space and his economic freedom. If a recession hits and Charles loses his job, he has a truck that can help him find another job. If he becomes ill, his paid time off will allow him to pay his bills while he recovers. If he needs food, there is money in his bank account. By these simple examples, it becomes obvious that property—whether in the form of a truck, benefits, or a paycheck—increases economic freedom.

Ten years ago, Charles was disempowered. Today, he's empowered. The difference? Property. Property and power are inseparable. In order for the poor to free themselves from poverty, both power and property should be privatized and protected.

The empowerment that Charles, April, Jocelyn, and countless others have experienced started with real compassion and inspiration that ignited renewed faith and agency. Those vital components to escape poverty are delivered through private charity as relationships are formed in the exchange. In the next chapter, we'll explore how some attempts to help the poor crowd out what caring community members can contribute, disrupting the natural formation of beneficial ties between compassionate helpers and people in need—ties that make communities strong.

CHAPTER 4

Charity Displaced

"LET THEM MAKE THE CUTS. We'll figure out some other way." The handful of community leaders around me, who had been discussing upcoming state budget cuts to prisoner reentry funding, were surprised at my declaration.

Maybe it seemed like I lacked the heart to help folks reintegrate into society after spending time in jail. Not at all. In fact, a significant portion of our mission's work is dedicated to helping these very people transition back into a life of work and independence.

No, my words weren't said out of a lack of care. Instead, I knew we would be able to continue our work helping these people without the government's assistance. And, as I suspected, when our governor cut $146 million from the prisoner reentry budget, a church in our community stepped up and began serving these ex-criminals with goods and services to prepare them to reenter the workforce. More than two years later, they're still actively involved in this ministry.

Did that local church know they were being crowded out of this opportunity to serve when the state was handling prisoner reentry? I believe the answer to that rhetorical question is key: What's crowded out is out of sight and therefore out of mind. More so, it isn't missed if it's filled with something else—in this case, the government's public spending.

In economics, the "crowding-out effect" is understood as the decline or elimination of private-sector spending due to a rise in public-sector spending. Each of the principles in this book has a clear connection to both liberty and charity. However, none has an impact as striking and concurrent as this effect. Simply put, when the government spends your resources for the sake of helping your neighbor, both charity and liberty take a synchronized blow. Your liberty is lost because your property is plundered for someone else, and your charity is diminished because your compassion is undermined by the subsidy your neighbor receives.

YOU DON'T GIVE TO A NEED THAT'S MET

Some question whether the crowding-out effect is real, and recent research has even attempted to debunk the theory.

If I gave you fifteen dollars and asked you to donate some to a charity of your choice, how much would you give? The answer is, "It depends." It depends on your perception—specifically, the perception of how much you started with before it was taxed. It's a fact proven by researchers Eckel, Grossman, and Johnston in a 2003 study published in the *Journal of Public Economics*.[1]

A group of 168 college students at St. Cloud State University in Minnesota were each given twenty dollars—well, almost. Half of them (group one) were given twenty dollars and then told a five-dollar tax was being levied on it to go to a charity of their choosing. They were then allowed to choose an amount they wanted to give to that charity from the remaining fifteen dollars. The other half (group two) were given fifteen dollars and told five dollars was already given to a charity of their choice, but they were *not* told it was a tax off the original twenty dollars. So both groups had fifteen dollars to work with, but group one knew they started with twenty dollars and then were taxed five dollars, whereas group two thought they started with fifteen dollars.

This simple research revealed a 100 percent crowd out in the group who knew they were taxed. In other words, whatever amount group two gave from their fifteen dollars, group one gave about half that much.

They didn't give less because they were less willing to part with their earnings; they hadn't earned a thing! And it wasn't because they had less money to give. The only variable was group one's knowledge that they'd been taxed.

Are you aware that you're being taxed? It might seem like a silly question—of course you're aware. But are you also aware that being taxed may make you less inclined to be charitable?

The St. Cloud study isn't the only research that backs this hypothesis. In fact, just knowing a particular social service sector is subsidized by government dollars causes most people to think twice before giving to it.

Researchers Jonathon Gruber and Daniel Hungerman discovered this in their research that examined church crowd-out at the advent of the New Deal's social welfare programs. They found that for every dollar the government spent in a particular social service sector between 1933 and 1939, church giving to that area of need decreased by at least 30 percent.[2] This amounted to a crowd out of about $385 million, which is equivalent to approximately $4 billion in today's economy.

Another more recent study on philanthropy revealed similar findings. More than one in ten donors stated that they would decrease giving if the government stepped in to support their charity, and nearly a third would increase giving if the government stepped out.[3]

It's not rocket science. You only give to a need that's not been met. If the government steps in to meet basic needs in our own communities, charity naturally declines. Government-sponsored poverty programs and personal charity don't mix well.

Let's examine this by looking at the correlation between free countries and their private giving habits. When comparing the Charities Aid Foundation World Giving Index 2018[4] with the Heritage Foundation Index of Economic Freedom from the same year, you'll find that of the top twenty

freest-ranking countries in the world ("free" defined as having a low tax burden, low regulation, and a free market), thirteen of them are also in the top twenty of the Giving Index (marked by levels of volunteerism, giving, and helping a stranger).

Considering there are 196 countries, the positive correlation is obvious. The flip side of that coin? High taxes and big safety-net programs make it a lot easier to pass by a neighbor in need. Simply put, you don't give to a need that's met.

YOU DON'T GIVE WHAT YOU DON'T HAVE

Pope Benedict in his 2009 encyclical *Caritas in Veritate* rightly positions charity as the greater virtue over justice:

> Charity goes beyond justice, because to love is to give, to offer what is "mine" to the other; but it never lacks justice, which prompts us to give the other what is "his"...[5]

He makes an important point that justice—giving a man what belongs to him (or not taking his property from him)—serves as the foundation for charity. Simply put, you've got to be able to keep what you've earned to then give what you have. Arguably, we've gotten this principle mixed up because we're seeing more and more promotion of socialist ideology: We're going to take what you have so we can give what we took.

But the reality is even worse than that argument because only a fraction of what's taken truly reaches the poor. The rest runs a giant bureaucracy. Our federal government has slowly drifted from one that protects private property to one that takes it. And once it's been taken, we don't have it to give.

How did this happen?

Less than twenty years after our nation's founding, a debate arose in the House of Representatives as to whether the US government should provide relief for Haitian refugees pouring into New England. They were escaping a war-torn Haiti in the midst of a revolution. The recordings of that third Congress reveal that compassion was the driving force in their consideration of whether $15,000 should be spent from the Treasury to aid the refugees. But James Madison's dissent was clear: "Charity is no part of the legislative duty of government. It would puzzle any gentleman to lay his finger on any part of the Constitution which would authorize the government to interpose in the relief of . . . sufferers."[6]

Was Madison heartless? Did his solid stance against federal government aid reflect an indifference to the suffering of others? Not at all. In fact, he pressed on to consider other ways to care for those refugees without compromising his principled constitutional position. For these early government leaders—the ones who had fought for freedom against the oppressive rule of a large and expansive government—their newfound liberty demanded the government they served remain small and limited. The state was to remain laissez-faire, hands-off in the affairs of men, providing only a simple framework of law and order upon which a free and flourishing society could be built—a society in which each person was unrestricted to speak his mind, build his dream, defend his family, and to be charitable toward his neighbor in need.

Today, just a handful of generations later, that strict constructionist and limited government perspective has given way to a contagious dependency on a massive federal system whose overreach feeds the masses but never solves the problem. Instead, true charity that flows out of compassion, selflessness, and love for neighbor is crowded out by a seemingly endless supply of state aid that too often incentivizes its recipients to remain sick and poor. What happened?

At the birth of our nation, the federalists argued for limited federal government and the anti-federalists petitioned for barely one at all. No one supported the notion of a federal government that would take the earnings of the individual worker to help the poor. And although there has always been vigorous debate concerning the rightful powers of our national government and the means by which to pay for their execution, there was a notable progressive and liberal political shift that took place at the turn of the nineteenth century.

Before that shift, Democrat Grover Cleveland took office as president in 1885 and set a record of vetoes in his first term (414) that still holds today. Why? As bill after bill made its way to his desk, he rejected many of them on the same grounds as what he articulated in his veto of the Texas Seed Bill of 1887, which proposed to help farmers through a drought:

> I can find no warrant for such an appropriation in the Constitution; and I do not believe that the power and duty of the General Government ought to be extended to the relief of individual suffering which is in no manner properly related to the public service or benefit. A prevalent tendency to disregard the limited mission of this power and duty should, I think, be steadfastly resisted, to the end that the lesson should be constantly enforced that, though the people support the Government, the Government should not support the people.[7]

But by 1909—just three administrations later—the shift had occurred. Republican Howard Taft took office with a different perspective on the role and reach of the federal government. In his first address to Congress, he proposed an amendment to the Constitution that would grant the federal government a new power to levy taxes on individual income. In regard to the 1895 Supreme Court ruling that struck down the first personal income tax law, he writes:

> The decision of the Supreme Court in the income-tax cases deprived the National Government of a power which, by reason of previous decisions of the court, it was generally supposed that Government had. It is undoubtedly a power the National Government ought to have. It might be indispensable to the nation's life in great crises. Although I have not considered a constitutional amendment as necessary to the exercise of certain phases of this power, a mature consideration has satisfied me that an amendment is the only proper course for its establishment to its full extent. I therefore recommend to the Congress that both Houses, by a two-thirds vote, shall propose an amendment to the Constitution conferring the power to levy an income tax upon the

National Government without apportionment among the States in proportion to population.[8]

In line with this advocacy of progressive expansionism, Taft formed the Children's Bureau in 1912 as the first federal agency to focus on improving the lives of children and families. That, in turn, led to the nation's first form of welfare, Aid to Dependent Children.

In a single generation, the guard of individual liberty was mortally wounded. Cleveland's small government ideas were pushed aside by a progressive movement that launched the first welfare program and, as never before, embraced the federal government's collection of personal income. And although that first income tax took only 1 percent from those who made more than $4,000 per year (about $105,000 today), it opened Pandora's box of government overreach. That same pattern now plunders personal income from three-fourths of America's families to support a trillion-dollar annual welfare bill. That's a trillion dollars you and I don't have to help our own neighbors in need.

But if we had it, would we really help our neighbors?

CROWDING IN

Imagine that my community received an extra amount of money from the US Department of Housing and Urban Development (HUD) in the form of a broad grant meant to develop the community, often referred to as a Community Development Block Grant (CDBG). Imagine that some local officials and city leaders came together to best determine how to use these funds.

Imagine that the group jumped on a bus and went through a few impoverished neighborhoods where they witnessed overgrown grass, half-dilapidated porches, fences in disrepair, junky front yards, broken windows, and a gross need to beautify rundown houses with a few coats of paint. Imagine that, after talking with a few of the residents, they returned to city hall for a meeting to discuss how to address the problems. They arrived at a plan to use the government money to fund an expansion of the parks and recreation division to include a "Community

Betterment" team. The grant would cover their labor and the cost of tools and equipment necessary to start knocking out the projects one by one.

I said "imagine" because it never happened. Our city did receive "extra" government dollars from HUD, but it used that money for something else. To meet the needs of our neighbors, who still wanted and needed help addressing those problems, our mission launched a program several years ago called Neighbor Connect, which connects one neighbor's skill to another neighbor's need. We developed a database system, populated it with hundreds of volunteers, including local businesses, and have staffed its oversight through private donations. Over the years, this decentralized approach of personalized charity has met thousands of needs in our community, ranging from assistance with personal finances and budgets to lawn care, car repair, and minor house projects, among many others.

In the end, it was to our community's benefit that those government grants didn't get used in my imagined scenario. It is unlikely that our mission would have sensed the demand to launch our Neighbor Connect program if the city had launched its Community Betterment program.

Remember, no one meets a need that's already met.

This scenario demonstrates an example of the crowding-out effect that could apply to nearly every town across America. Creative solutions lie in the hearts and minds of compassionate people. These unique ideas are waiting to be awakened from crowd-out-induced dormancy.

How many ideas? The number is immeasurable.

Edward Devine, a late nineteenth-century economist and pioneer in social work, was a child welfare advocate. However, his writings in his periodical *The Survey* revealed his belief that neighborly charity would rise up to meet most needs in the absence of any public support:

> If there were no social insurance, no public institutional relief, and no private organized charity—in other words, if there were no resources in times of exceptional distress except the provision which people would voluntarily make on their own account and the informal neighborly help which people would give to one

another, I firmly believe as Chalmers believed in Glasgow nearly three-quarters of a century ago, that most of the misfortunes would still be provided for . . ."[9]

I've witnessed that.

On Sunday afternoon, May 22, 2011, a supercell storm formed just southwest of our city. By the time it entered Joplin city limits, it had transformed into a mile-wide F5 tornado. After weaving a seven-mile path through the core of our community, it destroyed $3 billion worth of property. More tragic were the 161 lives lost, more than one thousand people injured, and more than seven thousand residents rendered homeless that day.

In the immediate aftermath and into the night, I helped pull people from the rubble as I looked for one of my own family members. Later on, I helped with wound care and continued cleanup, and my wife and I organized labor out of our mission. My kids were with us through the rescue, relief, and cleanup as well. This was not unique to our family. Thousands of other individuals and families did the same. Water distribution, extra shelter, medical relief, food, and clothing were provided by churches, missions, and neighbors.

One study reported that more than ninety-two thousand volunteers alongside 749 churches, charities, civic groups, and businesses contributed more than 528,000 hours to the recovery process. The same study reported that approximately 98 percent of the residents displaced from nearly seven thousand destroyed homes remained within twenty-five miles of the city. Most were with family and friends. It took weeks for the Federal Emergency Management Agency (FEMA) to arrive and help with some of these needs.

When they did, they set up just six hundred trailers as temporary housing, leaving more than 90 percent of the immediate shelter and temporary housing needs to be provided for by the private sector.[10]

When the government wasn't there, neighbors were.

Although neighborly compassion runs high during times of tragedy, it always has a steady flow. I've seen this in action, too.

About a decade before the F5 tornado, Housing First was in full swing. Housing First is an initiative that endeavors to first place homeless individuals in housing and then encourage them to independence with proper resources, medical attention, and case management. Housing First and its side-kick initiative, Rapid Rehousing, have been heavily funded and directed by the Department of Housing and Urban Development. Washington's "problem-solvers" pointed to this approach over the organic process of a person moving from the streets to a shelter and from a shelter to employment and from employment to an apartment. Thus, federal funding for emergency shelters was diverted to Housing First, which resulted in our local Salvation Army closing its family shelter.[11]

In the aftermath of that, our mission immediately experienced a spike in calls from moms and dads looking for shelter for their families. We had never thought about opening a family shelter until that moment. We launched an aggressive $1.2 million capital campaign, and a year later we had completed the renovation of an abandoned school building that would provide shelter for families.

When the government pulled its funding, the local community stepped up.

For years, homeless individuals in Topeka, Kansas were referred to a secular, government-funded work-ready program called Topeka Moving Ahead Program (TMAP). When the funding was pulled, a local nonprofit, the Topeka Rescue Mission, stepped up. As their director of education, Nell Ritchey, shared with *Instigate*, "When TMAP went away, we knew we had to do something to replace it." So they started CaRE, Career Readiness and Education Program. "The only difference," Nell said, "is that all the staff are Christians who exude Jesus wherever they go."[12]

Whether it's a prisoner reentry program, housing program, or work-readiness program, when the government pulls out, neighbors step in.

In the spring of 2017, a preliminary budget from the White House threatened to cut funding to the well-known Meals-on-Wheels program. Anyone who tuned into the news during that time heard cries of injustice condemning such a notion as an atrocity against the poor and elderly. Until that point, I had never thought of how our Neighbor Connect program could fill in a Meals-on-Wheels gap. After considering the possibility, our mission's team developed a plan that fit right in line with the purpose of Neighbor Connect. But instead of connecting a neighbor's mechanical skill to another neighbor's fix-it need, we began connecting one neighbor's cooking skill to another neighbor's food need. Now, for the last two years, our privately funded program has employed local church volunteers to successfully operate our own type of "meals-on-wheels" program.

Why did we launch this program? It was the government's threat to extract itself from an aspect of public charity work that compelled me to consider, "What can we do?" Consider again that when the government isn't there, neighbors are.

So, let's again consider the question: If we could keep the funds currently taken by taxes to pay for government welfare programs, would we really help our neighbors? I'm convinced we would. All of these examples of individuals and local groups stepping up to fill the gaps prove it. Government withdrawal from the charity sector would leave more in the pockets of compassionate neighbors, and the absence of public charity would create a vacuum for neighbors to exercise private charity instead.

Remember, we can't give what we don't have, and we don't give to a need that's already met.

In 350 BC, Aristotle corrected his philosophical predecessors by reminding the world of this truth:

> Again, how immeasurably greater is the pleasure, when a man feels a thing to be his own; for surely the love of self is a feeling implanted by nature and not given in vain ... And further, there is the greatest pleasure in doing a kindness or service to friends or guests or companions, which can only be rendered when a man has private property. These advantages are lost by excessive unification of the state. The exhibition of two virtues, besides, is visibly annihilated in such a state: first, temperance ... secondly,

liberality in the matter of property. No one, when men have all things in common, will any longer set an example of liberality or do any liberal action; for liberality consists in the use which is made of property.[13]

In summary, the common good is not served, nor is common liberality promoted in society by "all things in common," but more so by "each his own." Even in the fourth chapter of Acts, the followers of Jesus who contributed their goods, having "all things in common" did so willingly from property they owned. This pool of private property to meet needs in the community grew out of a common brotherhood, not government-coerced collection and redistribution. Aristotle would not be surprised today that socialism crowds out charity. But the crowding-out effect impacts more than our private property and the amount we give to good causes. As we discuss in the next chapter, it stymies the accumulation of social capital and the formation of neighborly relationships, which are vital for the poor to be free.

In the words of President Grover Cleveland, federal aid "encourages the expectation of paternal care on the part of the government" while it simultaneously "prevents the indulgence among our people of that kindly sentiment and conduct which strengthens the bonds of a common brotherhood."[14]

CHAPTER 5

Relationships Displaced

RELATIONSHIPS AND FREEDOM

The "bonds of common brotherhood" President Cleveland hoped to preserve and strengthen have suffered great abuse since his last day in office at the turn of the nineteenth century. Not only have government relief programs deactivated neighborly compassion, but the bonds within the nuclear family have been weakened or shattered. As welfare spending has increased dramatically since the 1960s (fig.1), so has the rate of children born outside of marriage (fig.2).

Government relief programs have reduced the need for interdependency that naturally occurs within marriages, family units, and local communities—a pattern that I qualify as a type of relational crowd-out.

Healthy relationships provide stability and opportunity, both staples of individual economic freedom. A colleague of mine once said, "A person doesn't become homeless because he runs out of money. He becomes homeless because he runs out of friends." Chronic homelessness and poverty are, at the root, much more about broken relationships than empty pocketbooks. Among the chronically homeless, these bro-

Welfare Spending by Program Type
TOTAL SPENDING IN TRILLIONS OF 2016 DOLLARS

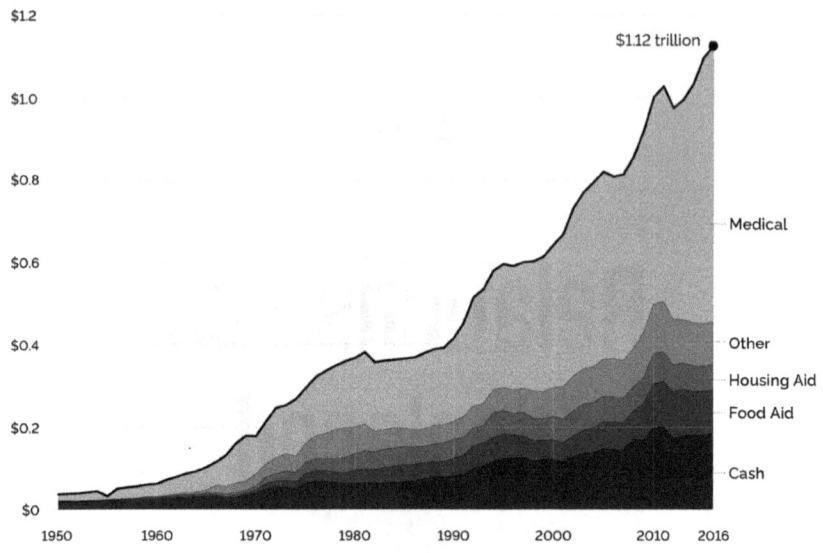

FIGURE 1

SOURCE: The Heritage Foundation, from current and previous Office of Management and Budget documents and other official government sources.

Graph adapted from The Heritage Foundation Backgrounder No. 3294, April 5, 2018, Chart 5, page 8

---

ken relationships extend beyond severed ties with family and friends to political disengagement and exclusion from the marketplace. I can't think of one person I've met in twenty years of street ministry who has been in healthy relationships in these arenas and is still homeless. Obviously, relational stability is an important factor in regard to America's problems of homelessness and chronic poverty.

There are three primary types of relationships: familial, marketplace, and political. Familial relationships shape social capital, marketplace relationships build financial capital, and political relationships influence social order. For now, we will focus on the importance of the first two, familial and marketplace relationships, because both impact economic freedom.

Marketplace relationships affect economic freedom directly through a free, mutually beneficial exchange of goods and/or labor. Healthy

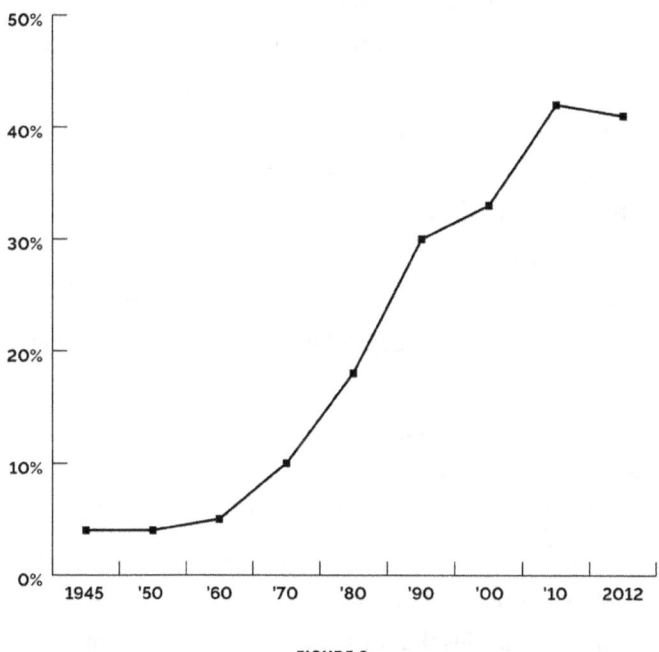

FIGURE 2

SOURCE: U.S. Department of Health and Human Services, Centers for Disease Control and Prevention, National Center for Health Statistics, National Vital Statistics Reports, http://www.cdc.gov/nchs/products/nvsr.htm (accessed September 10, 2014.)

Graph adapted from The Heritage Foundation Backgrounder No. 2955.

---

familial relationships impact economic freedom indirectly by providing a safety net in times of crisis. These are not always distinct categories. For example, we hire a variety of individuals to work in our ministry (marketplace relationships). Two of those employees' lines blurred from coworkers to friends when they started dating, and later they entered into a familial relationship when they married each other. Similarly, businesses often bridge market-based relationships to craft an environment of trust and become more like family by incorporating recreational activities, food and drinks, and other social events at business functions.

Just like businesses, the distinction between familial and marketplace relationships can be blurred in the church. Relationships within a church are categorized first as familial—more relational than transactional—but may bridge into meaningful marketplace relationships. This is one of the great social benefits of the church as an institution, that it becomes a unique stage for familial relationships to develop between people who differ widely. Because the church speaks to issues common to all people, regardless of wealth or status, it is the most likely platform for relationships to be developed, which benefits those who are unlikely to find themselves in a common place on such common ground.

Social scientist Robert Putnam describes the difference between bonding and bridging social capital in his popular book, *Bowling Alone*:

> Bonding social capital is good for undergirding specific reciprocity and mobilizing solidarity.
>
> ... Bridging networks, by contrast, are better for linkage to external assets and for information diffusion. Economic sociologist Mark Granovetter has pointed out that when seeking jobs—or political allies—the "weak" ties that link me to distant acquaintances who move in different circles from mine are actually more valuable than the "strong" ties that link me to relatives and intimate friends whose sociological niche is very like my own. Bonding social capital is, as Xavier de Souza Briggs puts it, good for "getting by," but bridging social capital is crucial for "getting ahead."[1]

"Getting ahead" is getting free. If our charity is to empower people toward their own economic freedom, building these relational bridges is vital.

If bridging social capital is "getting ahead" and bonding social capital represents "getting by," should we frown on the latter? According to social capital researcher and sociologist Xavier de Souza Briggs, not at all. In his paper "Brown Kids in White Suburbs: Housing Mobility and the Many Faces of Social Capital," he shares the results of a study in the late 90s that compared the social capital changes of black families who moved from poverty to a housing development in an affluent neighborhood to the families who remained in the impoverished neighborhood. Although the research revealed no significant differences between the two groups, Briggs clearly discusses the importance of the support provided through bonding-type social capital:

> When we turn to other people to help us cope with challenges that life presents, from flat tires to divorces, social capital is at work. When poor moms share caregiving tasks or rides to church, or when they reinforce norms that support job search along networks of relatives, friends, and acquaintances, they each draw on social capital in its support guise.[2]

At first, it may seem odd that the families who moved into more affluent neighborhoods failed to increase bridging social capital. The researchers noted, however, that the youth of these families stayed on the grounds of their housing development, and families still attended the church in their old neighborhood, which only facilitated bonding-type capital.

What's the big deal? If you're poor and unemployed, bonding with others who are poor and unemployed doesn't lead to a job. In contrast, hanging around people who are employed increases information about potential work opportunities and therefore improves your outlook for employment.

Briggs comments on his findings:

> Most striking and worrisome is the fact that over one-quarter of all the adolescents cannot think of a single significant adult in their lives... whether kin, acquaintance, or friend, who would be a good source of information on getting a job. And in direct corroboration of Wilson's (1987,1996) arguments about social isolation and the effects of joblessness on young people of color, knowing just one employed adult or one white adult (and these categories are correlated) dramatically increases the chances that the young person will report at least one reliable source of job information in his or her network of active adult ties.[3]

How would his findings have altered if the churches in the immediate area had engaged the families in these new housing projects? What if a local charity made an effort to form relationships with these newly transplanted families? The church as an institution can transcend racial and socioeconomic differences, making it a likely establishment for a young, poor, unemployed adolescent to shake hands or break bread with an employed professional. Local charities also hold this potential if the volunteers and staff are focused on relationship development more than just meeting superficial needs.

Our mission's metrics fall under three primary categories: career, character, and connection. That last category drives us to creatively consider ways to re-establish or facilitate new relationships with our neighbors in chronic poverty. Ultimately it led us to develop mentoring tools, training, and outreach opportunities for potential new members. We also encourage our staff to model a lifestyle of connection.

Jerry is one of the people I connected with. He's a thirty-two-year-old homeless man recently released from prison, tall and thin with tattoos on his arms, no teeth, and a speech impediment. It was our second meeting and our first lunch together at a local BBQ joint when he shared more of his background. His father was abusive. His older sister ran away when she was sixteen. His twin brother threatened to kill him after he couldn't make payment on a drug deal. He shared all this in stride, eating his pulled pork sandwich, like a guy who's learned to roll with the punches. He went on, "I'm trying to get back on my medication."

"Medication?" I looked into his clear blue eyes—the eyes of a thoughtful and drug-free man. "Why do you need medication?"

"To get my housing. I also need to get my SSI check started again now that I'm out of prison."

"Jerry, you don't seem disabled or sick to me. Maybe you just need a job." I started casting the vision. "Consider what it would be like to just get a job, save up your money while you stay in our shelter, then move out into an apartment and be completely independent." He stopped eating. I could tell he was contemplating.

"I do like to wash dishes," he admitted, recalling a job he once had at a restaurant. A few minutes later, while my wife was engaging Jerry, I slipped out of the booth and made my way to the restaurant's hostess stand. "I just started mentoring this guy," I pointed back at my table, "and he just told me he used to work as a dishwasher and enjoyed it. He needs a job. Got anything?"

"As a matter of fact, we do."

Jerry walked out of our lunch that day with an employment application. He interviewed later that week and got the job. I loaned him some money to buy his uniform of black size thirteen no-slick shoes and three black t-shirts. He had an excellent—and confident—first day with his hands in soapy water.

Jerry's shift away from welfare and subsidized housing started with asking him one question when we first met at the mission: "Hey, what's your name?"

This type of personal connection can be sparked at churches, missions, and charities, which represent an incredible opportunity to develop social capital. Currently, larger cities, especially ones on the West Coast of the US, are experiencing incredible difficulties with chronic homelessness. Certain areas are overrun with trash, tents, and human waste. Locals cry foul, "Not in my backyard!" Housing advocates plead for more vouchers from the federal government. State officials vote for more funding for mental health services. Even the Trump administration sent a team to California in 2019 to examine the problem, only to end up pointing a finger at shelters and declaring the message that more people would find housing if shelters didn't exist.

I've been working in this field long enough to attest that homelessness isn't solved by housing vouchers, mental health services, or shelters. None of these Band-Aids will improve economic mobility toward freedom more than someone intentionally walking down Skid Row, under a bridge, or through the doors of a shelter, and asking, "Hey, what's your name?"

Because *bonding social capital* provides a natural safety net to help someone "get by" (instead of falling behind) and *bridging social capital* helps someone "get ahead," both should be nurtured and developed to aid economic stability and mobility. Does our public policy interrupt these important relationships? Yes. Have our social justice intentions backfired by crowding out the relationships that are key to empowering the poor? Yes. Why are our good intentions missing the mark and interfering with effective solutions?

RIGHT DIAGNOSIS, WRONG PATHOLOGY

The number one thing we're doing wrong is misunderstanding pathology. Yes, the diagnosis is "poverty" or "homelessness," but those diagnoses do little to explain the nature of the underlying cause, the pathology. Missing the pathology of chronic poverty and homelessness often results in simple but ineffective Band-Aid-type treatments. In fact, I once saw a sign from a national organization with a mission to end homelessness that read, "A housed person isn't homeless." Although this is obviously true by definition, it can be equated to saying, "A person's open wound isn't open when it's covered with a Band-Aid." As a wound care specialist with a decade of practice, I know that simply covering a serious wound with a mere bandage can complicate the problem, resulting in a deeper infection or an abscess. The same is true for government initiatives for subsidized housing. Providing a roof over a person's head doesn't address their underlying issues of broken relationships.

Josh is a good example. I was taking a nonprofit leader on a tour when we rounded the corner to our mission's dining room. We ran into Josh, a student in our long-term program, and I asked if he'd share a bit of his story with our guest. He said that he'd received a HUD housing voucher for one year, so he spent the previous year in government housing. "For a year, I didn't work, and I got in a lot of trouble. Then I got evicted. I should have been here the whole time. This is what I really needed."

It was good to develop a relationship with Josh and help him move toward self-sufficiency. Sadly, that relationship development (and the healing of some serious wounds) was delayed a year because of the government's good intentions. The diagnosis of "homelessness" had been addressed with a house instead of relational care and accountability to address the pathology.

Or consider the story of Seth, a young man in his twenties. One day, he was having lunch at the mission, so I sat down with him to talk. "What brought you here? How'd you land in our shelter?"

"Well, I was living with my mother and my grandmother. Things were tough there, and an agency in town told me that if I'd live at the mission for a little bit, they'd get me free housing."

It's stunning, isn't it? This agency's solution to Seth's situation was separating family members in order to provide free housing. Unfortunately, I've seen that type of relational crowd-out effect far too often. This breakdown of the family often starts when local organizations apply for and receive government grants with a specific target. For example, one federal housing grant, "Shelter Plus Care," comes with this rule: "By regulation, the grantee must serve at least as many participants as shown in the application. No program change is permitted in this regard since the amount of funds originally awarded was based upon this number."[4]

It's no stretch to imagine the pressure case workers feel when their organization wins a grant like this. You get the money, and now you have to find clients who need it. Casting a net to find those clients isn't intended to separate families or trap people in dependency, yet that is often the outcome. When the government steps in to help a particular class of people, it naturally creates an incentive for individuals to qualify. And like all means-tested programs, the poorer you are, the more likely you are to qualify. Because healthy relationships increase your social and financial capital and decrease your likelihood of qualifying, the tendency is to cling more to the state and less to family. It was that unintentional but perverse incentive that drove Seth from his family to homelessness. He hoped to qualify for a free house.

TEACHING THE IMPORTANCE OF FAMILY

Trading the cure (relationships) for the Band-Aid (government aid) has failed to address the pathology and has instead propelled generational poverty. After twenty years of serving the homeless and impoverished,

I'm currently engaging a generation of younger people who seem to have lost sight entirely of the purpose of relationships and family.

One day, I stepped outside the doors of our mission to see an angry young man wildly waving a piece of paper over his head. He was stomping and yelling, "They can't do this! How can they do this!"

After talking him down, I asked him to share the reason for his angst. "This paycheck," he showed me the piece of paper he'd been waving radically, "look how much they took!"

I immediately responded, "Taxes?"

"It's not just taxes! They took half my check for child support!"

I naturally kicked into teacher mode. "Well, if you have a child, shouldn't you support him?"

"Yeah, but I didn't know they would take half my check! Someone should have told me this before I had a kid," he grunted.

I thought I'd heard it all in my twenty years of urban ministry, but that statement caught me off guard. I gently asked, "And who should have told you?"

He thought for a moment before shrugging his shoulders, "I don't know. I guess the government."

As soon as he said it, I knew I'd never forget it. I learned later that his father was in prison and his family was broken. Somewhere along the road of poverty, neglect, and family dysfunction, he started to believe that the state should teach him and that the government would save him—not rob him.

"Is Caesar our savior?" Eric Laverentz asks in his book of the same title. Laverentz, a Presbyterian minister, argues that the state has taken on the role of caring for the poor, a task that belongs rightfully to Christ's church. More importantly, he asserts that the church has transferred that responsibility to the government but should take it up again: "We rightfully recognize and respect Caesar's God-appointed responsibility and authority—but not at the cost of our own."[5]

The fact that the young man thought Caesar should have warned him is indicative of family or relational crowd-out. It's not the government's job to teach the young man the importance of abstinence or birth control or any other aspect of sex-ed. That's the job of parents, of family. But the more Caesar teaches our kids and the less we educate them ourselves, the more our kids will turn to Caesar for answers. We already see this happening. It is the motor propelling generational poverty.

It's natural to assume that impoverished parents would teach their kids how to escape poverty, but many of those parents have not been taught to strive for independence. Their parents didn't know it either. This is, in part, due to a cultural shift surrounding the stigma of welfare.

George Segall's sculpture, "Depression Breadline," depicts men standing in line for food during the 1930s depression. It's iconic of poverty in this era: men in their hats and coats with dropped chins and downcast eyes. The sculpture is not imaginary; it's based on real men during a time of intense poverty and neediness. One of those men in line said, "Shame? You tellin' me? I would go stand in the relief line [and] bend my head low so nobody would recognize me."[6]

That stigma of dependency has changed.

Several years ago, soon after our mission had joined the Association of Gospel Rescue Missions (now Citygate Network), I was invited to Colorado Springs for a national meeting of mission CEOs. During one of the mealtimes, I sat at a table with a handful of others and mostly listened. I was the "new guy on the block" and simply wanted to absorb all that I could. At some point, the conversation turned toward the business of day-to-day operations. The guy to my left said, "Yeah, but it all slows down on Mother's Day." The others chuckled. I was lost. Mother's Day?

The Urban Dictionary definition of Mother's Day is the day of the month when welfare checks are issued. The inference is disturbing. First, it infers that mothers don't need husbands. The state will provide. Second, children aren't gifts. They are little people who translate into dollars. Finally, it celebrates government dependency rather than personal responsibility. The state now pays for being dependent.

The stigma has changed.

The increase in government transfers to the poor is a solvent that has weakened the glue of family and communal ties. With the government crowding in, Josh doesn't need the help of a gospel mission, Jerry doesn't need a mentor, and Seth doesn't really need his mother. This disruption not only negatively impacts a person's bonding social capital but displaces the responsibility from relationships to the government.

State aid is not the only culprit. Thoughtless charity has the same effect. Feeding America, one of the nation's largest privately supported charities, boasts that it provides more than four billion meals every year to Americans. Because of the charity's tie to special tax credits, all donated food must be given away without any aspect of reciprocity or exchange.[7] Rather than investigating existing family relationships, who should be the first source of help, food pantries accepting Feeding America donations are encouraged to simply give away the food, no questions asked.

Although local charities are more likely to strengthen the natural ties of family and community, they too can be guilty of relational crowd-out. One food pantry director in a nearby community, fed up with Feeding America's requirements, called me a few years ago. "I'd really like to get away from using their food," she said. "It frustrates me that I have to give it away without asking questions." When people become numbers, restrictions will continue to steer toward crowding out relationships instead of true charity.

It's not just a problem for government-funded entities, either; even our privately funded mission has been guilty of crowding out relationships. We received a request from a widow whose roof was leaking. We employed a friend from a local church to assess the issue. The report came back that it would require a team for at least a full day. Under our guidance, this church partner assembled a compassionate crew and even purchased the materials for the repair. They spent an entire Saturday fixing her roof.

I followed up with the team afterward for feedback on the project. "It went very well," the leader reported. "The only thing that was a little bothersome were the two grandsons who looked to be in their twenties. They sat on the couch watching football all day instead of helping." We missed out on that one. Had we investigated more, we would have known she had family members who could (and should) have been a part of helping. The excitement of potentially helping a widow brushed due diligence aside and, rather than strengthening family ties by calling the grandsons into action, we crowded them out.

Whether it's big government, big charity, or just bad charity, good intentions often interfere with the communal ties that exist naturally in families and communities. These vital relationships lend to proper accountability, stronger bonding social capital, and improved chances for developing relationships that form bridges for people to escape poverty.

I'll conclude this topic with a clear warning from Alexis de Tocqueville in his *Memoir on Pauperism,* which contrasts the benefit of individual charity to build social capital versus the relational detriment from public welfare, which he calls "legal charity":

> ... individual alms-giving established valuable ties between the rich and the poor. The deed itself involves the giver in the fate of the one whose poverty he has undertaken to alleviate. The latter, supported by aid which he had no right to demand and which he may have had no hope of getting, feels inspired by gratitude. A moral tie is established between those two classes whose interests and passions so often conspire to separate them from each other, and although divided by circumstance they are willingly reconciled. This is not the case with legal charity. The latter allows the alms to persist, but removes its morality. The law strips the man of wealth of a part of his surplus without consulting him and he sees the poor man only as a greedy stranger invited by the legislator to share his wealth. The poor man, on the other hand, feels no gratitude for a benefit which no one can refuse him and which could not satisfy him in any case ... Far from uniting ... the rich and the poor, into a single people, it [legal charity] breaks the only link which could be established between them.[8]

That "link" is the primary route for most who escape poverty. If a relational bridge does not accompany a transaction, the transaction remains a form of relief only rarely translating into freedom for the individual.

INTERLUDE

The Parable of Iustitia

THERE ONCE WAS A VILLAGE nestled at the base of a great mountain. For several generations, the community thrived. Homes were filled with laughter, relationships were cherished, and new vocations were embraced.

But, in time, a darkness came over the place—a hovering cloud that never left. Many citizens became disgruntled, discontent, and envious.

One morning after a fresh snow had disrupted the haze, a visitor was spotted coming down the mountain face. The chancellor assembled his council to discuss the stranger, who was still days away from descending into the village. An unwelcoming wariness met the man when he finally arrived.

Instead of formal introductions, the chancellor asked, "From where did you come?"

The man, unassuming and of no great stature, grabbed the lapels of his fur coat and hiked his shoulders to bring it around his neck. "Iustitia," he said, pointing toward the peak.

The city leaders knew of Iustitia. Stories of the place were so common they surpassed typical folklore. Tales of Iustitia were woven into children's books, holiday celebrations, and family dinner conversations. They all conveyed a common theme: that the unseen city was their homeland, a place on the other side of the mountain from which their ancestors had come generations ago. It was said to be a gleaming city where all things were right; where there was no want, no hate, and no crime.

Puzzled, the chancellor asked, "What brings you from Iustitia? Surely you saw the dark cloud that covers us as you crested the mountaintop."

"I did," the stranger affirmed, "and I've come to invite those who are both desirous and willing to come back with me over the mountain to my home—our home."

Our home. It sounded nice to those who were tired of life in their depressed city. One by one, they looked up at the mountain face, past the tree line, to the snow-covered peak, the cap of which was covered by a drifting cloud. *Our home* seemed out of reach—too far, too exhausting, too dangerous.

The stranger smiled, a glimmer of light in the grim, concerned crowd. "Come with me," he encouraged. And though that smile conveyed warmth and a glimpse of better times, they all walked away, certain that the distant hope on the other side of the mountain was out of reach.

All, except one.

This one man implored the stranger, "Wait, please wait. I'll be right back." He returned with a dozen people, ranging from very young to very old. "We want to go," he told the stranger. "My family, we all want to go." Every person in the group nodded their agreement. In the background, the other villagers watched, waiting to see what the stranger would do.

For a moment, he looked them over as if to size each one up for the task. "This won't be easy, and I'm not sure all of you will make it because the journey is long and difficult. Listen to me: There is no shortcut."

No one in the family flinched. The motley crew was committed.

And so, following the mysterious stranger, the group set out on the journey, leaving the gloomy village behind. Before the day was up, they had broken through the dark canopy covering the village and began their slow ascent up the mountain's face.

As the first day came to a close and the group stopped for the evening's rest, they strained their necks to see the mountain's top. It seemed like they hadn't ascended at all. Their lungs were strained. Their legs ached. Their hearts pounded. But they had never been happier.

Back below the dark canopy, the council gathered, freshly motivated by this mysterious hiker claiming to come from the place they had only known as an elusive legend. Maybe it *was* real. Each of them admitted a fire had been lit in their minds and hearts to somehow reach Iustitia. But they didn't want to follow the experienced hiker on the strenuous journey. They thought that they could devise a better way to reach Iustitia. The sun closed the day, but the council lit their lanterns to continue working on plans through the night—plans for a shortcut.

The following morning, the rays of the dawning sun struck the mountain face with power, urging the hiker and his disciples to rise early, pack up camp, and resume the climb. For them, the day was filled with fishing, fires, laughter, and labor. At the end of it, the patriarch of the family looked toward the peak and thought maybe they had made at least a little progress toward the summit.

While the family progressed, the council convened. The twelve of them had worked through the previous night until they came to a consensus on a plan to reach Iustitia more easily and efficiently. It would require the enlistment of engineers and general laborers, and the remaining labor and supplies would come from a new tax under an ordinance they called the Iustitia Exploration and Restoration Tax Act. Resistance to this funding measure was minimal. Most were either too mired in apathy to push back, or they favored the government's attempt to make the situation better. If a shortcut was possible to a different life than the one they were living, a tax hike was welcomed.

Weeks later, the sounds of explosions and tunnel boring began. The plan was underway to bore under the mountain to the other side, creating a subway to Iustitia—a shortcut.

Meanwhile, the ascending family neared the peak. Throughout the journey, their lung capacities had expanded, and red blood cell production had increased to meet the demands of less oxygen in the thinner air. Their clear eyes, stronger bodies, and healthy skin revealed the benefits of the daily climb over the last month.

Yet the advantages of their time on this mountain extended beyond the physical changes. Gratitude was common as they each willingly traded their service of mending for cooking or cooking for carrying. Joy marked the evenings around a fire filled with music and stories. Most of all, they were at peace. No one was disgruntled, discontent, or envious. They were, in fact, in no hurry. As night fell, so did the flames, leaving only the glow of embers. The family slept peacefully, unable to hear the churning and grinding of a giant drill at work far beneath them.

Their renewed energy carried them to the summit. As the family and the hiker crested the peak, they stood on the ridge to take in the view. The family was surprised. Where they had expected to see a heavenly city lighting the valley far below, there was nothing but tall, waving grass. No city, no buildings, no roads, no people.

The patriarch turned to the hiker. "Where's Iustitia?"

The hiker took him by the arm and began to descend. The family followed until they came to a large, flat outcropping of rock. "Step out to the edge and look with me," the hiker encouraged. They closed the gap until they could take in the mountainside around them.

The elder of the group said, "Look, a fire. And I see some people." Another family had set up camp nearby on a small plateau.

Someone else pointed, "Look! Over there. It's another group!" The team pivoted their gaze to find another congregation around the edge of a small lake. Suddenly, they realized they were far from alone.

The hiker smiled. "Sit down, please. Let me explain." The family found natural seats on rocks beside the peak, as the wind gently blew. "When you began this journey with me, what was it you thought you might find?" They looked at one another, each hoping someone else might bite.

Feeling some sense of responsibility, the man who had convinced his family to come finally spoke. "Well, I don't want to give an oversimplified answer, but—"

"Then don't," the hiker interrupted. "Tell me in detail what you expected."

The man nodded and said, "I was expecting to see a beautiful city, one with no darkness over it, where people are happy and free, a place where violence is restrained and justice reigns. I expected to see a place where people are smiling instead of depressed and where life isn't so hard—"

The hiker interrupted again, "Do you mean a place where life is easy?"

"Okay, maybe not easy, but good." He thought to himself. "Yeah, good. Where people work hard, but treat each other fairly. A place where the fruit of work is owned by the worker and shared out of compassion. Yeah, that was my hope for Iustitia."

The hiker looked in silence at the man. It was a waiting look, one of those with an expectation; not so much an expectation that the man would continue speaking but that some revelation would suddenly enlighten him.

The man considered what he had just said, his want, his hope, for Iustitia. The hiker slowly smiled, looked at each person in the group, and then toward the other families now starting their evening fires, sharing their laughter and music across the mountainside. He then turned with his back to them and stretched out his arms as if to try and hug the huge expanse before them.

Then the revelation came. They *had* found Iustitia. But it wasn't the Iustitia of the books they had read, nor was it the place they had ever pictured. Instead, the hope for that perfect city had been realized on their journey.

The man uttered the revelation as it fell on him. "Iustitia is not a place to live. *It's a way of life.*" The hiker spun around with his arms still wide and a smile on his face. "Welcome."

Nearly five miles below them, the tunneling project was nearing a breakthrough. Hundreds of government-paid laborers had been working around the clock in shifts. And though the project had suffered delays, ranging from union negotiations for better wages to various health and safety violations, they had successfully driven the giant drill through the base of the mountain.

As the first beam of daylight shone through the last layer of rock, the drills were stopped. The foreman wiped his brow, removed his mask, and spit dirt that had somehow found its way in. "Okay, go get him." Immediately, another worker in an electric utility cart spun around, turned on his yellow flashing light, and headed back to the city to pick up the chancellor. The chancellor had demanded it. He wanted to be the first to step into Iustitia; the first to welcome his people into the brilliant new city; the first to be seen by the citizens of their new home.

The chancellor stepped into the vehicle and the dirt-covered driver congratulated him. "You did it, sir," he said as he sped into the tunnel under the mountain.

Everyone in the city had their bags packed and boarded the public transportation buses paid for by the Iustitia Exploration and Restoration Tax Act. They began motoring under the mountain, excited about the new life they had been promised. As the community gathered beside the drill, which remained poised to open the passage to their new and glorious life, the chancellor grabbed his megaphone.

"My people! Whether you were in favor of this endeavor when we began or not, we have arrived, and you are about to be the recipients of the fruit of our successful plan. In a moment, I will turn this drill back on, and we will complete our passage to Iustitia, the legendary city of our forefathers. I asked not what you could do for us, but instead have worked to do this for you."

He flipped the switch.

Eyes wide with great anticipation, the people crowded toward the drill as it broke through to reveal their utopia. The emptiness they stepped into was so shocking that it took more than a minute for it to set in. Hundreds of people spilled out onto the grass, looking all around and even into the sky, as if the majestic city might be hovering above them.

There was nothing.

They were silent. The realization began to settle on them like a great weight.

From the overlook, the family saw it happen. The tip of the giant drill pierced the last layer of rock and began protruding into the space far below. They watched the people from under the mountain flood out onto the green grass where there was no city. They appeared as ants so far below, and after a moment, they could no longer be seen once the black haze also emerged from the tunnel to cover them again.

All their efforts to reach an end were lost. After all, there is no shortcut.

CHAPTER 6

The Heart

IUSTITIA IS THE LATIN NAME for Lady Justice. If you recall from chapter one, we generally defined justice as "what ought to be." The parable of Iustitia illustrates that the end we hope for—what we believe is right and just, what ought to be—is only reached through sacrifice, effort, and solidarity that is rooted in compassion, responsibility, and real relationships. In other words, there are no shortcuts.

In part, this is because justice for the poor cannot be neatly packaged in the vision of a decent home, consistent income, and a reliable vehicle. In a way, that was what the Iustitia townspeople expected to find on the other side of the mountain. But we know the end of the story.

Iustitia wasn't just an end; it was also the means. The same is true when we're discussing justice for the poor. Sacrifice, effort, and solidarity that is rooted in compassion, responsibility, and relationships are more than means to an end—they are the very components of a flourishing life, "what ought to be" for us all.

It's time to transition from problems to solutions, from philosophy to application. Although the upcoming chapters represent a framework for solutions, they are not intended to be an exhaustive, all-encompassing practical guide. That's another book.

Instead, we will bridge the heady information from part one with the hands-on information in part two. But first, we must recognize what lies between the head and the hands: the heart.

There are endless philosophies to consider, models to try, programs to implement, or reform bills to pass. Yet without connecting love for others with the virtue of charity, America will remain in want of the reform it so desperately needs.

Every few months, a handful of students from our men's long-term recovery program spend a week with me and my wife. We have morning devotions together, eat together, work outdoors together, and enjoy time fishing, throwing horseshoes, or laughing around a campfire. These men all meet the standard definition of poverty, but there's no sign of that during our week together. It's seven days of sacrifice, effort, and solidarity rooted in compassion, responsibility, and relationship. These means to an end become an end in itself—justice.

This isn't easy but it's beautiful. It is to desire *being with* more than *doing for*.

Bruce gets this. He lives in White Clay, Nebraska, with his wife, Marsha. They founded a ministry to help the Lakota Natives on the reservation in Pineridge, South Dakota. This particular reservation is one of the most impoverished areas in the Western Hemisphere, rivaled only by Haiti.

Once, Bruce and I were in his truck heading north from White Clay to Pineridge, and he was lamenting the constant barrage of short-term mission trips. He said something I've remembered for years: "James, I want people to stop coming and *doing for* the Lakota people. I want them to come and *be with* the Lakota people."

After living there for years, Bruce and Marsha have learned that good intentions often result in a lot of activity, but that *doing for* rather than *being with* is a means that falls woefully short of justice.

Bruce and Marsha have the hearts we all need—hearts to trade short-term, long-distance mission trips for short-distance, long-term relationships. And it is in those relationships that we get close enough to understand the real need. There are no "distant" fixes for poverty.

"Pits" also understood this. The last time I visited the Vietnam Veterans Memorial, I was there to see one specific name on a wall of 58,318 names memorialized for the ultimate sacrifice they paid on the battlefield: William H. Pitsenbarger, or "Pits."

On April 11, 1966, thirty-five miles east of Saigon, twenty-one-year-old United States Airforce pararescueman William Pitsenbarger was lowered through the trees by a helicopter into a firefight where injured Army soldiers were pinned down. He tended to their injuries and helped soldiers into the lift basket. When the helicopter began taking on enemy fire, the pilot called Pitsenbarger to return to the chopper, but Pits waved him on, remaining with the other wounded soldiers, improvising splints and stretchers out of vines and saplings. It's estimated that he saved sixty men that day before he was shot and killed by a Viet Cong sniper. Pitsenbarger knew the only way to help these men was to be in the fight with them.

Dumping aid from a chopper would have been futile. Sure, they could have simply dropped crates of bandages, tourniquets, and morphine syringes, and then they could have flown away saying they did something *for* the injured. But Pits knew that in order for each soldier to receive what he really needed, he needed to be *with* them. Each man required individualized triage for his unique injury. In other words, to *do for* them well, he had to *be with* them first.

The same is true for impoverished individuals. There is no way to shortcut the process of helping people out of poverty. Ultimately, it requires someone who desires "being with" before "doing for."

Unfortunately, our country and communities have a tremendous number of energetic planners who want to do something *about* poverty more than they want to be *with* people in poverty. And as long as that inversion persists, the poor will never receive the relational inspiration or the social capital required to escape poverty, they will never be welcomed into circles where new opportunities are born, and they will never be encouraged toward avenues that create wealth.

None of that can be delivered from a hovering helicopter. To know what's really needed requires that we're close to the person in need.

We need a primary desire to *be with* more than *doing for*. Because *doing for* is an attempted shortcut while *being with* is the long hike to Iustitia.

After working for more than twenty years to help people out of poverty, I can assure you that there's no shortcut to justice. There is no shortcut to install character or fortitude. There is no shortcut to prepare a person for work opportunities. And there is no shortcut to building relational trust in someone who has only known broken relationships.

But striving for those things—character, work, trust—as social ends can lead to both rhetoric and policies that support shortcuts. After all, it's easier to achieve good character if we lower the bar in our schools through curricula that justifies victimhood. It's easier to lift wages through sweeping legislation than to develop work skills. And it's much easier to substitute government dependency for trustworthy neighborly interdependency.

There is no shortcut, yet too often we look for one.

Why? Maybe we lack the right heart for the person in poverty and for the liberty he deserves.

THE PRICE OF LIBERTY

Every Memorial Day, I reflect on how more than a million American men and women have paid the ultimate sacrifice on the battlefield in the name of freedom. There is worthwhile debate concerning whether we justly entered all seven of those conflicts for the cause of freedom, but aside from the arguments, I admire those who died, fighting with the intent to protect and serve our liberties. The fact that we have such liberties is certainly worth celebrating! However, the rapid rate that we're losing them is sobering—or it should be.

How do we maintain freedom? To answer that question is part of this book's objective. And as the parable demonstrated, there are no shortcuts. When I consider the great cost of our liberty, I arrive at this conclusion: The successful maintenance of liberty is dependent on the recipient's willingness to die for its preservation. In other words, a free people in a free land who value their liberties above their lives will maintain both. However, a free people in a free land who value their lives above their liberties will eventually lose both.

For many, the idea of elevating liberty above life resonates well. For others, such statements are nothing more than quips that provoke a roll of the eyes. Let's not be too quick to judge those dissenters. After all, there is an apparent paradox in the idea of dying to preserve something you cherish. Does it ever make sense to sacrifice for something you cherish if your sacrifice separates you from that very thing? When would you be willing to pay such a price?

When it's done for the love of someone else.

IN THE NAME OF LOVE

Someone will willingly sacrifice only when the importance of preserving liberty for posterity exceeds the risk of dying. Such a willingness is born, then, from a mix of two things: understanding man was meant to be free, and a love for family, friend, and neighbor. However, if either of those reactants is missing from the formula, the product can never be the preservation of liberty.

Let's say that someone thinks he should be ruled and restrained by leaders who are more fit and powerful. By failing to believe that man is naturally entitled to be free, he won't embrace a willingness to die for the liberty of another.

However, if he saw the right to freedom as naturally inherent to man, he may be willing to die for the liberty of another. But he still must love his neighbor.

In fact, both the love of liberty and the love of fellow man are conjoined in a symbiosis of sorts. Consider freedom to be the rightful robe thrown about the shoulders of a man. If I do not care about the man under the cloth, then why would I sacrifice myself so that he may be clothed in the robe? I cannot care about the garment unless I also take note of its rightful owner. I cannot care about the man and be content with him naked. And if there is no man, the robe is just a useless garb. No, the garment of freedom and the man it cloaks are either both cared about or both ignored.

VISIONARY VS. UTOPIAN

Too many people too often ignore both. When people believe that a just social end can be delivered through public policy, it is much easier for those people to lose interest in liberty and the love of neighbor.

This is the result of a utopian pursuit. Its chase is as common as its elusiveness. In fact, this Latin word we've come to consider synonymous with paradise literally means "no place." Utopia is no place, yet it has been pursued by regimes and subcultures in every generation. Man's quest for it stems from an inherent, subconscious familiarity with perfection. As creatures made by an unerring God, we have an ancient elemental understanding of perfection in contrast to imperfection, right versus wrong. Our very hope to be in the right stems from a day long ago when there was no wrong, no error, and no poverty; only peace and prosperity. We innately desire to be there—utopia.

In the parable of Iustitia, both the family who went over the mountain and the city leaders who went under it had the same hope for the future: a community flourishing in peace and prosperity. But the family members were visionaries while the town's authorities had a utopian mindset.

The difference is that a visionary sees the required path to reach the destination, but a utopian perspective only sees an end with no boundaries on how to get there. The visionary is motivated by progress, whereas the utopian's motivation is dependent upon a lack of it. The visionary is diligent to pursue logical steps along a clear path, whereas the utopian is ruthless, caring only about the end. He gives way to heartless measures to reach his goal, whether that be drilling a shortcut under a mountain or passing a massive piece of legislation to cure poverty.

The principled visionary, however, considers good character, hard work, and mutual trust to be the primary components that help reach peace and prosperity. Isn't it safe to assume that most people in America today want good character, hard work, and mutual trust in our society? In general, we want people to flourish in a vocation and to lower unemployment. And we want families to be able to trust their neighbors and even strangers.

Character, work, and trust. In the parable, these sought-after characteristics came alive to the family on the summit. Yet those who tried the shortcut found themselves despairing. And if a nation despairs long enough, its people become disillusioned, then despondent, and ultimately dependent. To retain our freedom—and for the poor to be freed from poverty—there is no shortcut.

So, who climbs this mountain? Who cleans up the homeless encampments? Who cares for the mentally ill wandering our streets? Who deals with the addiction within the walls of HUD housing complexes? We all do, the poor included. But in the next three chapters, I specifically want to address three institutions: charitable practice, philanthropy, and public policy. Taken together, our concerted efforts to reshape these three establishments—if guided by the right heart—could transform the landscape of poverty in America.

CHAPTER 7

Smart Practice

WHETHER YOU'RE A CHURCH PASTOR, missionary, lay ministry leader, church volunteer, social worker, social service agency leader, charity organization volunteer, or just a Good Samaritan, the principles that guide your practice of charity matter. As a charity practitioner myself, I am keenly aware of the difficulties of this work, which makes me even more grateful to serve the poor alongside you.

Obviously, none of us has figured out the best way to help the poor. We will always be shifting from best practice to better practice. Our posture of humility is the welcome mat that invites a healthy challenge to our ideas and ultimately leads to reformation. Like a kind and gentle soul who opens his door to a stranger, humility welcomes unknown truth for more than just a brief stay. In other words, we accommodate truth.

Reckoning with the detrimental effects of my practice of handout charity was a moment of accommodation. When I realized that it was more harmful than helpful, truth was knocking at my door! I had a choice: I could either lock the door and walk away, or I could open it and welcome the wisdom and change it would bring. Pride always wants to lock the door to protect our old, comfortable ways and ignore that there may be a better way to do things. Humility is the inquisitive character whose door is always open, secure in an environment of trial and discovery.

As we continue to seek a more effective way to help the poor, there are three foundational principles that I believe distinguish excellent charity and ought to form the backbone of poverty alleviation: authentic charity, accurate charity, and actualized charity.

AUTHENTIC CHARITY

The luxury watches made by the Swiss company Patek Philippe, founded in 1839, range from $10,000 to more than $1 million. If you're like me when it comes to watches, then you would have a hard time telling if someone was wearing an authentic Patek Phillippe. How would you know the difference between a genuine and a knock-off? The Stern family, which has owned the company since 1932, would say there are a lot of differences. They are intimately aware of the construction and components of every watch made by their brand. They care about their meticulously crafted pieces much more than the company that made the mass-produced one I wear on my wrist.

In fact, one of the easiest ways to tell that my watch isn't genuine is because it doesn't have a certificate of authenticity. A certificate of authenticity tells us where the item comes from—its source. For Patek Philippe watches, the certificate does not just certify that the watch didn't originate in one of the countless factories of cheap watches; the document certifies that it came from the Stern family in Geneva, whose craftsmen laboriously create and construct each timepiece by hand, focusing on every minute detail. Ultimately these practices have proved its invaluable, time-tested quality compared to its mass-produced counterparts.

If we designed a certificate of authenticity for our charity, what would it say? Authentic charity is real help from compassion-ignited individuals who desire to make a difference. Is there a knock-off version? Absolutely. It may resemble true charity, but the source will likely be an institution or bureaucracy forcing people to contribute.

All certificates include the source, and the proven source of effective charity is compassion. Unlike mass-produced attempts to meet the needs of those in poverty, compassion creates an impetus for a personal, hands-on approach to charity. With compassion as the source, the subsequent methods and direction of charity can be handcrafted with that specific individual's unique background, needs, and talents in mind.

This source of compassion is vitally important because poverty is complex. Arthur Brooks in his book *The Conservative Heart* differentiates complex from complicated. He describes the building of a jet engine as a complicated problem, but once the problem is solved, the same steps can be followed to build one jet engine after another. He likens a complex problem, however, to that of a football game. No matter the tools of predictive analysis, no one can know with certainty the outcome of a game or reproduce it. It's too complex.[1]

Likewise, the lives of people who have been struck by poverty are too complex for a single one-size-fits-all solution, and no bureaucratic blueprint plan can mass produce a solution for individuals in need. As we've already seen, we need to see charity derived from real compassion and not compulsion. The legislated redistribution of others' wealth through government programs to help the poor should be the absolute last resort for many reasons, but one of the biggest is that it has simply failed to deliver sustainable solutions.

For the last fifty years, the official poverty measure hasn't improved; it has only toggled between 11 percent and 15 percent (fig.1). If anything, poverty has grown worse as more impoverished individuals have actually grown poorer. The share of those in deep poverty (below the 50 percent poverty line) has been increasing since 1975 (fig.2) and today, 48 percent of all those in poverty are in deep poverty.[2]

Why has massive government spending failed to substantially decrease poverty? Because government programs are not authentic charity. Programs funded by the government don't stem from the compassion of individuals who really care about their neighbors in need. Therefore, those programs can never adequately address or even determine the root causes of poverty in the lives of uniquely different individuals.

Private, compassionate funding of charity is nothing novel. Only in the last one hundred years have we seen a shift to address poverty through impersonal mass redistribution. For most of history, charity

FIGURE 1
SOURCE: U.S. Census Bureau
Graph adapted from UC Davis Center for Poverty Research: https://poverty.ucdavis.edu/faq/what-current-poverty-rate-united-states

has been authentic—compassion calling one person to help another. It is the natural arrangement of individuals in families and families in communities. Shouldn't a parent be the first one to help his or her child? Isn't it better for a neighbor to help his neighbor before the government helps his neighbor? Should a community look for a state grant before calling on its churches and civic organizations to solve a problem?

This pattern—family helping family first, then helping neighbors and their community—is a principle called subsidiarity. In essence, matters ought to be handled at the local level by those who are most competent and closest to the need. It was formally introduced in Pope Pius' encyclical *Quadragesimo Anno* in 1931.[3] He wrote, "Just as it is gravely wrong to take from individuals what they can accomplish by their own initiative and industry and give it to the community, so also it is an injustice and at the same time a grave evil and disturbance of right order to assign to a greater and higher association what lesser and subordinate organizations can do."

Share of the poor in "deep poverty", 1975-2012

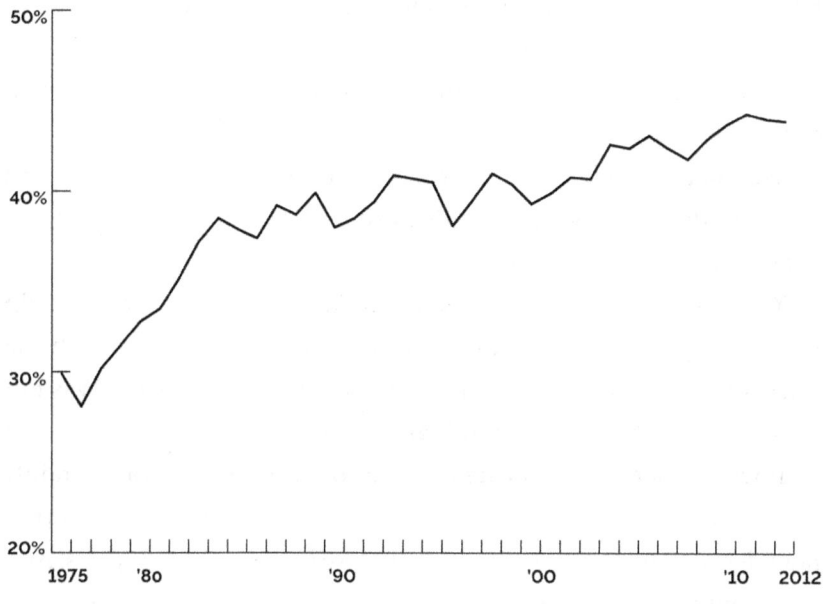

FIGURE 2
SOURCE: Authors' analysis of Current Population Survey Annual Social and Economic Supplement Historical Poverty Tables (Tables 2 and 22)

Graph adapted from Economic Policy Institute, "Already More Than a Lost Decade": https://www.epi.org/publication/lost-decade-income-poverty-trends-continue/, figure H

Subsidiarity and authentic charity go hand in hand because when we're close to a person in need, we're more likely to feel compassion for him—and remember, compassion is what certifies your charity as authentic.

Most importantly though, respecting subsidiarity through the practice of authentic charity is more effective. Why? Because when you're near to the person in need, you tend to know more about him. That knowledge equips you to render effective, knowledgeable, compassionate, and tailored help.

Supporting and practicing authentic charity helps all of us hit the mark of what's really needed to help a person toward a flourishing life. And hitting that mark is all about accuracy.

ACCURATE CHARITY

A man named Jason used to come and go from our mission. Sometimes he stayed in our shelter. Other times, he would just come for food or clothing. I remember one specific day when Jason was sitting in our foyer eating peanuts. He was leaning back in the chair with his baseball cap on, legs casually crossed.

"Hey, James, come here," he waved me over. Curious, I obliged, and he proceeded to say something I'll never forget: "You guys make it way too easy for us to stay homeless."

You can imagine how shocked I was. All of our efforts were to help get Jason *off* the streets. But his comment made me wrestle with the question—could our help be keeping people *on* the streets? Was our charity hurting more than helping?

It wasn't that we didn't care about Jason. Our charity was certainly authentic. We had compassion for him and the thousands of other homeless and impoverished people that we had engaged for years. And our genuine compassion had driven us to do a lot. But I had to reckon with the truth that our charity—even with all its good intentions and diligence and effort—was failing to empower people. It was missing the mark. Simply put, it wasn't accurate.

Accurate charity is charity that's centered on the heart of the matter. One very easy way to understand accurate versus inaccurate charity is to consider the difference between a plastic childhood dart and a professional metal-tip dart. A kid's dart is flimsy and difficult to aim, complete with a poor-quality suction cup at its end. It's tough to shoot because that plastic was not made to soar more than a few feet through the air; that same reason makes it nearly impossible to aim.

However, if you do manage to hit the target, it will likely bounce right off. If you're lucky enough to make it stick, it probably won't remain there for long.

In contrast, a metal-tip dart is sleek, weighted, and perfectly pointed to pierce the bullseye. Its textured grip and lightweight body ensure an accurate throw. No matter how far away you stand, it is capable of hitting the very center of a small target. And when it does, it penetrates.

Consider charity work from the perspective of accuracy and impact. The early years of my fighting poverty were more like aimlessly tossing a plastic dart instead of strategically throwing a metal one. My varied efforts were scattered, never accurately reaching the center of the target or penetrating to the heart of the matter.

What does it mean for charity to hit the center of the target or get to the heart of the matter? Well, that's different for everyone, because each of us is unique and complex with our own specific histories and present situations. But regardless of the endless differences among us, there is one thing that's common to us all. We all have a center, a core identity—who we are as a unique, valuable person. The heart of the person is our target.

Accurate charity not only reaches the heart but respects it as well. Respectful charity upholds the uniqueness of each individual, reinforcing a person's distinct identity by empowering him out of poverty. When Jason told me that we made it too easy for him to remain homeless, what I heard was, "You're not respecting or upholding my unique abilities to help me escape poverty!"

Accurate and respectful charity takes a lot of effort. And that's challenging. But if we limit ourselves to the child's dart approach, we will never call the person we care about to apply himself, and we will never really get to the heart of the matter.

Therefore, accurate charity always favors reciprocity, an exchange. Reciprocal charity is more accurate because the person is not just on the receiving end of our good deeds. He or she is giving back—reciprocating—which helps us understand the strengths, weaknesses, and other unique attributes of the person we're helping.

If you think about it, reciprocity is natural. Each of us is specially made in the image of our Creator. The Latin term for this is *imago Dei*, meaning the image of God. Because we are made in the image of our Creator, we ourselves are also intended to create. This means we're naturally producers more than we are consumers. Our charity fails to be accurate if we only feed the consumer side of a person. Even more, we should focus on the producer side, rightly regarding the imago Dei in every person by re-awakening ability, motivation, and hope in the people we help. When we do this, our charity becomes more effective than a superficial, plastic-dart approach.

By respecting someone's unique gifting through the healthy expectation of reciprocity, accurate charity reaches the heart of the matter. It is the most likely way to truly empower a person to liberate himself from the chains of poverty. That's the result we're all hoping for, and it's one worth measuring. And measuring results is the only way to note if our charity is actualized.

ACTUALIZED CHARITY

Pause and dream with me. Consider some of the advances in civilization that now magnify our leisure, equip us to work, or connect us in ways that seemed impossible not long ago.

In the 1800s, a young German boy named Karl Benz grew up in poverty. If he hadn't dreamed of an easier and faster way to travel, he may have missed his grand invention of the first automobile. At the turn of the century, we took flight. That, too, required someone like the Wright brothers to boldly dream of a way to join the birds of the air. And eighty years later, someone held a phone in their hands for the first time... without a cord attached to it. A man named Marty Cooper sat in a Motorola lab, dreaming of how to make that a reality, and now the cell phone has revolutionized how we communicate and access information. Grace Hopper dreamed of the modern-day computer, and then she programmed it. Jonas Salk dreamed of a cure for polio, which has nearly eradicated it.

It's important for us to dream too. If you were to dream about something for your city, what would it be? No homelessness? No hunger? No unemployment? There's no end to the good dreams for your neighborhood, city, state, and beyond. Dream big—and then do something with it.

Yes, there are barriers. There are things that can stand in the way and prevent our dreams from actualizing or coming true.

One of the first roadblocks is the principle of competitive inhibition. It's why two trees don't grow too closely together. There simply aren't enough nutrients in the earth to feed two trees from the same plot of soil. Physical pain signals are similar. When we are injured, we rub our skin. This sensation competitively inhibits the pain from being transmitted to our brains. Both signals can't occur at the same time.

Our dream capacity follows the same pattern. It is natural for us to imagine things that have yet to be created, to dream. However, when we are occupied with external stimuli from news, social media, or entertainment, our brain becomes a receiver rather than a producer. The stimuli competitively inhibit imagination and the formation of dreams, plus our ability to pursue them.

So, my first admonition? Turn it off. Let your own mind wander rather than scroll through someone else's. Don't let your dream machine be crowded out by yet another Netflix binge.

Second, I want you to believe. Dreaming about a more virtuous or prosperous city is one thing. Believing it's possible is another. If we don't believe that a community problem can be solved, a social ill can be cured, or an institutional injustice can be righted, then we will never put our hand to the plow. In fact, dreaming without believing is the forerunner of utopianism. In contrast, believing that our dream can come true launches our vision with a plan. Will we be ridiculed? Maybe. Will our dreams be questioned? Probably.

I dream of a day when the poor and hungry in America are fed through private means—local charities, churches, civic fundraisers, and, most importantly, employment. I shared that at a 2021 US congressional hearing as the only witness opposed to the expansion of SNAP, the Food Stamp program. Congresswoman Alma Adams of North Carolina asked me, "Do you really believe that forty-two million Americans currently dependent on the SNAP program could be fed by the private sector?" Yes, I do.

I was being ridiculed. For what? For believing that the private sector is better capable of taking care of neighbors in need than a massive, bloated federal government. It's a dream, and I believe it's possible. My belief drives me toward that mark with a strategy to bolster the private sector through education, training, and tools. I work to inspire the electorate to motivate philanthropy to support civil society's response rather than the government's.

Let's dream, but let's also believe there's a route for it to come true.

Finally, measure your progress. Even when our belief motivates us to action, that activity may fall far short of the impact we hope to have. This happened during my early years of ministry. There was a lot of activity, but I was far from supplying a real or lasting impact in the lives of the people we were helping.

So, how do you know if you are progressing in your vision for your church, ministry, or city? In charity work, we tend to count meals, the number of people we shelter, or how much money is raised, and then we guess at how much progress that means we've made. But actualized charity goes beyond a hunch, and those who practice it do more than count output from their programs.

Actualized charity is outcome-driven, meaning we need to measure markers of real impact along the way.

This naturally occurs when we consider our charitable work from the perspective of building a vision. Constructing what we hope for involves measurements along the way, just like constructing a building involves measurements along the way. A bricklayer does more than count the bricks he's cementing to erect a wall. He also measures angles and trajectory to make sure that he is actually achieving the vision: a strong and straight wall.

What you and I are doing day in and day out may be feeding people, sheltering individuals, or even helping them through classes. But if the vision is for people to feed themselves, provide for their families, and contribute to their communities, then we should measure indicators of self-reliance, family stability, and gainful employment. Those are outcomes that, when achieved, are more likely to bring that vision to fruition.

Actualized charity is charity that actually makes an impact, and the only way to know is to measure markers of the impact you hope to make. So let's have a dream, a vision, and a plan, and then let's measure our progress along the way.

CHAPTER 8

Wise Philanthropy

IN 2001, UNDER THE LEADERSHIP of President George W. Bush and Mel Martinez, US Secretary of Housing and Urban Development, the US Interagency Council on Homelessness was reactivated with a new objective: to coordinate federal resources to end chronic homelessness within ten years. Obviously, they failed. In fact, homelessness across the nation has increased 5 percent over the last few years to nearly six hundred thousand people.[1]

But at the time the council was reactivated, there was a significant national movement to encourage cities to form ten-year plans to end homelessness, and ours was no exception. At that point in my ministry, I had learned the importance of collaboration and had been connecting scores of nonprofits in my city via a web-based tool. This allowed our community's charitable network to share real-time information regarding the help people were receiving. So I was excited about the opportunity to deepen that collaborative effort around a plan to end homelessness.

A group of fifteen leaders met monthly at our city hall. It was a diverse crowd representing individuals from city administration, law enforcement agencies, hospital administration, shelter operators, and other nonprofits. "Tara" was one of those nonprofit leaders, a woman employed with our local Community Action Agency.

Community Action Agencies were created in 1964 as part of Lyndon Johnson's Great Society plan; of those that are still around today, more than one thousand of them remain mostly government-funded. As co-chair of the committee tasked with developing a plan for addressing homelessness in our city, I was pushing hard for our plan to be funded voluntarily through private means. But when the plan developed to include the construction of a residential center to help homeless individuals with their addictions, Tara grew concerned that we might fail to raise the funds necessary to implement and execute the idea.

I remember sitting across the boardroom table from her as she expressed her doubt. I answered it with optimism, expounding on the importance of an inspiring vision paired with an actionable plan as the catalyst for donor support. More than twelve years after that conversation, I can still clearly recall the perplexed look on her face. "I've never really thought about that," she said. Comparing my response to her own work at the Community Action Agency, she went on, "The programs we develop are dependent on the stream of funding we receive from the federal government."

For those of you wanting to donate to fight homelessness, understanding this dichotomy that Tara described is important.

First is the unfortunate reality that some nonprofit leaders are too willing to accommodate the demands of the government for the dollars they offer. We'll discuss more of those character and policy issues in the next chapter, but for now, it's enough to understand that the tradeoffs this accommodation can require might hamper an organization's efforts to help others.

Second is the equally important reality that as much as I think my inspiring vision is worthy of private financial support, if donors don't give, my vision remains a vision only.

So, bottom line, nonprofit leaders are either aligning with government or with private philanthropy (or some combination of the two).

HOW TO KNOW WHICH ORGANIZATIONS TO SUPPORT

As a matter of principle, only support the poverty-fighting efforts that align with your convictions. In the last chapter, I encouraged nonprofit leaders to practice the three tenets of true charity to avoid trapping people in dependency. Now, I encourage you to support those organizations and practitioners who carry out those tenets of true charity. Financially supporting poverty relief efforts that trap people in cyclic poverty is akin to aiding and abetting generational injustice.

But how can you know what your money will be supporting? There are certainly watchdog agencies like the Better Business Bureau, Charity Navigator, Evangelical Council for Financial Accountability, and many others. However, most of those deal with financial integrity and transparency rather than outcome measurements and reciprocity. That means you may need to do some research on your own. Here are three questions to ask a nonprofit leader before offering your financial support.

What does your program require of its clients?

Adam Smith, often referred to as the father of economics, made a very simple but profound observation, which he recorded in his seminal work, *An Inquiry into the Nature and Causes of the Wealth of Nations*. In his explanation on the evolution of division of labor, he wrote, "Nobody ever saw a dog make a fair and deliberate exchange of one bone for another with another dog. Nobody ever saw one animal, by its gestures and natural cries signify to another, this is mine, that yours; I am willing to give this for that."[2] Of course, the voluntary exchange Smith describes is a characteristic of humanity and markets. So consider this: If we strip a person of his opportunity to exchange something he has for something he needs, then do we also strip from him some aspect of his humanity?

To require something of someone when they are in need is a method that can preserve human dignity. Sure, there are times when one-way relief with a distinct provider-receiver dynamic is appropriate. Natural disasters, house fires, and other sudden losses should be met with compassionate, open-handed charity—but not for long. As soon as adequate shelter has been provided and a meal served, it's time for your favorite nonprofit to expect something in return from that client. Otherwise, continued handouts signify the person has nothing to contribute and is destined to be continually dependent on a system of charity or welfare.

How can a nonprofit ask a person for something in return? They can help out with chores around the facility. Clients can work a certain amount of time to earn vouchers, which can be used to meet their needs for food, shelter, and clothing. They can even set and meet specific goals, like creating a résumé or applying for jobs. Once you hear about the requirements, be sure to ask, "How?" This simple question helps you understand the extent and quality of the nonprofit's operations.

Is your program restricted by other funding?

Our mission was once offered half a million dollars. It was intended to be seed money toward a $2.5 million brick-and-mortar project to help the addicted in our community. The problem, however, was that the money was offered by our city government. Although it was promised with "no strings attached," our mission had never received government money and was wary to do so. To understand more, I called Jim, a Salvation Army leader in another city. I explained the situation and, without any reservation, he shot me his opinion over the phone: "Don't do it."

"Wow," I replied. "That was quick. Why do you say that, Jim?"

He then shared a story about when he accepted a Community Development Block Grant (CDBG) from the Department of Housing and Urban Development to build a cafeteria dining room addition to their ministry. He, too, had been told "no strings attached." However, after construction was complete and they had opened their doors, the American Civil Liberties Union (ACLU) was notified that they were praying in the new facility. The ACLU then sued them. Jim was exasperated as he reached the end of his story: "Now we can't even pray over our meals in that section of our building!"

Jim was unaware of a few important lines buried in Title 24, Part 570 of the Federal Code: Organizations that are directly funded under the CDBG program may not engage in inherently religious activities, such as worship, religious instruction, or proselytization, as part of the programs or services funded under this part. Although this has been updated in the code and is worded slightly differently, it still imparts the same restriction. Jim just wanted to pray out loud in his cafeteria. Unfortunately, it really wasn't his to pray in.

You may want the nonprofit you support to have the freedom to pray. You may not care. But it's important that the nonprofits we support have the freedom to address problems and serve the unique needs of their clients. Recall in chapter five the story of a food pantry that was unable to withhold food, even if it was the right thing to do. Their hands were tied because of an IRS rule dealing with tax credits. They're not the only ones.

Feeding America has dozens of locations across the country. The one in southwest Missouri regularly distributes food to fifteen nearby food pantries, including the one I mentioned in chapter five. Our mission refused to take their food because accepting it meant that we couldn't ask people to work for it. In an effort to reach a compromise, we asked if we could set goals with clients who received the food. "No," was their response.

A local reporter interviewed the CEO of that specific food bank about the situation. He responded, "... the criteria that is mentioned specifically under Section II [of the IRS code] is that 'the property is not transferred by the (donor) in exchange for money, other property or services.' We have to follow federal law just like everybody else."[3] He's correct; the IRS does restrict tax-deductible donations from being exchanged for "money, other property or services."[4] Unfortunately, that line is interpreted to mean that nothing can be asked of the client in need. This is happening every day at locations all across America, trapping millions of people in food dependency instead of liberating them through healthier partnerships, esteeming them to exchange something they have for something they need.

The food pantry I mentioned in chapter five grew so tired of having their hands tied—forced to give away food with no questions asked—that they finally stopped accepting any resources that would constrain their ability to love people by coupling food with relationship and accountability. That's the type of food distribution ministry I encourage you to support. If an organization is taking government money or resources that hold it back from practicing effective charity, consider if its overall effectiveness warrants any private support at all.

Does your program measure outcomes, or simply outputs?

I was once asked to speak at a fundraising banquet for a ministry in a neighboring city. In hopes of grabbing a story to share in my remarks, I unexpectedly stopped in to talk with some of their clients. My wife and I were welcomed and quickly seated at a four-top table in a large room styled like a restaurant, buzzing with volunteers taking drink orders and running plates of food. They served us tea, rigatoni, a side of green beans, and warm French bread. I wasn't even hungry, but feeding is what they did. I read their mission statement on a table tent, "A Compassionate Community Feeding the Hungry," and recalled the information promoted on their website's front page, "More than 2,000 free meals served each month."

Like countless poverty-fighting organizations in our nation today, they measured output, not outcomes. Weeks before I had arrived there for my meal, I got to know their leadership team and that they wanted to make some healthy changes in their organization. They wanted to measure long-term impact, and I was sure the comments I heard around my table that afternoon would reinforce their desire. The couple across from us at our table kindly remarked, "We drive from another town simply because it's a free meal." The table beside us chimed in, "At least we don't have to cook when we come here." It sounded like the folks around me needed a free meal as much as I did (which was not at all). The leadership realized that two thousand free meals served each month really wasn't that meaningful.

We all need to realize that—especially donors.

Imagine how ludicrous it would be if a business gauged its success on production outputs alone. No manufacturer celebrates units made more than units sold. Similarly, it is also absurd to celebrate needs met more than lives impacted, but it's a common practice. So why do we see output displayed so often in the nonprofit sector?

Two reasons. First, measuring human impact isn't easy. Counting food boxes or classes completed is easy work, but tracking how those same food boxes or completed classes translate to a better life is not simple.

Second, some programs simply don't connect to meaningful outcomes because there's no outcome to measure. This was the case with the ministry I visited. Later that year, as they went through our outcomes training, they realized their free-meal-service program could not be tied to any meaningful measure of progress or advancement in the people it was serving. I'm happy to report they're in the process of changing their model to include a check-in activity and life skill classes to begin tying meaningful impact to their programs—and measuring it.

When you ask your local nonprofit leader this particular question about outcomes, listen for one of these common outcome domains:

- Employment
- Housing
- Education
- Social networks
- Family stability
- Health
- Financial stability

And then reply with a very simple request: "Can you show me how you measure them?" Likely, they'll pull up a spreadsheet or an outcomes-tracking software. Taking time to study this will not only confirm what you need to know to offer your support but your time and attention will communicate that you care about the hard work that goes into measuring outcomes.

AN OPTIONAL FOURTH QUESTION

The three questions we've just discussed—What does your program require of its clients? Is your program restricted by other funding? Does your program measure outcomes, or outputs?—are simple to ask but immensely valuable in gauging an organization's effectiveness. To many,

I'm sure I sound like a hardnose for suggesting that you ask these questions. But once you see the incredible benefits of people being recognized and treated as more than mere recipients of others' charity, you'll understand the importance of supporting a nonprofit that strengthens individual agency and builds personal autonomy.

I would also encourage asking a fourth question: How can I help you achieve your objectives?

Many leaders I meet want to change their model to be more reciprocal, and I've had many conversations with leaders who would like to get away from government funding. Those who are fighting poverty for more than accolades embrace the idea of measuring their impact more accurately. Your financial support, accountability, and volunteer time may encourage those nonprofits and churches to improve their effectiveness.[5]

According to *Giving USA*, nonprofit work in America was supported by $471 billion of private philanthropy in 2020, a 5.1 percent increase from 2019.[6] That's a remarkable amount of financial partnership that, if stewarded in harmony with the ideas in this chapter, could be a tremendous force that brings real solutions to the problems of poverty.

CHAPTER 9

Embracing Policy

I AM A PRACTITIONER. TO a lesser extent, I'm also a donor. I am not, however, a policymaker. Nonetheless, I have realized the influence public policy has on my work as a practitioner as well as the direct effects it has on the poor. As a result, I have become more interested in the role of government as it relates to poverty. Though my experience is minimal, the weight of policy in this space is so great that I am compelled to address it in this final chapter. While the previous two chapters directly addressed the practitioner and the philanthropist, here I humbly address the electorate—not the policymakers, but those whose vote impacts the policymaker and therefore policy itself.

"Politics just aren't my thing." That's a common sentiment these days, especially as the federal government continues to expand beyond its constitutional boundaries, magnifying the disconnect between policy and the impact of a vote. However, whether we feel we can have an impact on policy or not, policy impacts us. It may not be "our thing," but we're certainly "its thing." We can't escape it because we're social creatures, which also makes us political creatures.

Aristotle points this out in *Book I of Politics* as he argues that the individual is set into a family, families into a village, and villages into the state. This arrangement might remind you of the term "subsidiarity" that we discussed in chapter seven, the idea that situations should be handled by the smallest and nearest association before a larger, more distant one is employed. Aristotle notes the same concept, ordering these natural relationships by connecting a person to the state. He concludes that man is a "political animal" who exists inside this natural political framework because anyone who is somehow isolated from it must be "either a beast or a god: he is no part of a state."[1]

If Aristotle was right, then the natural, interdependent relationships between individuals within a family are as important as the connections between families and their village and equal to the relationships of villages with their state. You and I are inextricably linked from our daily lives to the life of our government. To somehow escape that is personally and socially detrimental for, as Aristotle notes, such a scenario would degenerate us into beasts who think we are gods.

The state is not the source of civility—that comes from God and the convicting guidance of his Holy Spirit. The very presence of conviction signals both a world in need and humanity composed of opposing individual wills. And so incivility and injustice are options. For this reason, the apostle Paul defines the primary purpose of government in his epistle to the Romans, noting that authorities "are God's servants, agents of wrath to bring punishment on the wrongdoer" (Romans 13:4, NIV).

But even if no one did wrong, would we still live in a world without government? Without *polis* or greater communities? Without cities? Even in the end, there will be a city of God, a New Jerusalem, that is ruled by a perfectly just and benevolent King. There will always be a regime of one form or another, and as much as it will promote civility, it will also promote *politeia* or policy.

Aristotle was right. The civilized and political are inseparable. We are political creatures. Therefore, we have both a personal need and a social responsibility to understand the policies that impact our lives, families, communities, and especially our neighbors in need. We should not abdicate with a shrug, "Politics just aren't my thing." Instead, we need to commit to making it our thing. It matters. And here is how you can make it more of a central part of your fight against poverty.

READ, WRITE, AND SPEAK UP!

Take thirty minutes every morning to read the papers. Yes, papers. Whether physical black and white sheets or digital screens, read your local news and a national paper every day. Of course, not every article will be relevant to the mission of addressing poverty, but before a week has passed, you'll likely learn something that will inform your work as a volunteer, an employee, or a donor.

In the middle of 2020, I read an article in my local paper reporting on the previous evening's monthly city council meeting, which included the city manager's address to the council. He had just completed a city-wide listening tour and shared the key points that he felt needed to be addressed. One of those was homelessness, with a focus on panhandling. I reached out by email sharing my willingness to serve, and I was called on to help.

So, I took two of my team members to meet with the city manager and some of his staff. Together, we established a plan to raise funds for billboards, radio announcements, and television ads that directly focused on panhandling. The result? A notable reduction in panhandling. This partnership was a successful private solution to an issue that our city government felt it needed to address. Not only did we free people from being stuck on a corner holding cardboard signs, but we were able to serve our city leaders and raise more awareness about our charity work.

Here's the point: None of that would have happened if I hadn't read my local paper. What kind of influence could your habit of newspaper reading have on your community?

Staying informed also helps you address current events through opinion editorials (op-eds). It's not easy to compose a meaningful article in five hundred to seven hundred and fifty words, but it can make an impact. For years, we've developed great partnerships with new donors and volunteers who read our op-eds. It may seem like expressing your opinion in a newspaper has little effect, but if no one wrote about the importance of individual dignity through work and how that intersects with compassion, charity, and justice, then readers would only hear the opposing view. And all that's heard is often all that's known.

More importantly, though, your words have the opportunity to influence voters in your area—and even national voters if you're published in larger outlets.

Be brave with your words, like a young man I met, Juan Montesdeoca. As a cosmetology student in Arizona, Juan had been fined because he was cutting the hair of homeless vets without a cosmetology license. Homeless individuals testified to how thankful they were for his service, and he expressed how much he enjoyed serving. Yet bad policy got in the way of his helping the poor. Juan wasn't quiet about it. He called a news station and amplified his concern about this injustice. The news reached the governor's office, which then influenced the state board of cosmetology to stop their pursuit of penalizing Juan. Better still, Juan was willing to share his experience with policymakers around the nation, resulting in a closer look at regulations that may unnecessarily restrain "good Samaritan" acts and pathways to professions.

In his work *On Liberty,* the nineteenth-century political philosopher John Stuart Mill points out the importance of opinionated expression:

> Unless opinions favorable to democracy and to aristocracy, to property and to equality, to cooperation and to competition, to luxury and to abstinence, to sociality and individuality, to liberty and discipline, and all the other standing antagonisms of practical life, are expressed with equal freedom, and enforced and defended with equal talent and energy, there is no chance of both elements obtaining their due; one scale is sure to go up, and the other down.[2]

Consider your opinions concerning policies that impact poverty. Is your opinion currently on the scale that's up or down? Public opinion is influenced by expressed opinion. If you're not writing and expressing your opinion in the public square, those who elect our policymakers may only know one side. Take the initiative and inform them of yours.

BUILD RELATIONSHIPS

We've talked a lot in this book about the power of building relationships with those in poverty, but building relationships with folks in the policy space is also important. Your government representatives need to hear from you, and a relationship opens the door to being heard.

There are a myriad of ways to connect with people in the policy world. Our region hosts "Eggs and Issues" to connect our chamber of commerce members with local representatives over coffee and breakfast. Maybe your community has a regular town hall that serves the same purpose. Candidates want their voices to be heard, so watch for events around election times. Set time aside to go and listen, but also to introduce yourself and your cause.

However, here's a tip I've learned from experience: Many legislators think the introduction of a social justice cause will quickly be followed by a request for money. When I first met Tom, a state congressman who was also state treasurer at the time, I had set up an appointment with him to share about our True Charity Initiative. For about half an hour, we sat at a table in an ice cream parlor on the town square where we discussed the impact that well-intended yet bad policy was having on the people we were helping at our mission. More than a few times, he asked leading questions that made it seem like I was asking for him to include our charity in the upcoming budget cycle. Confused at the misunderstanding, I finally said, "I don't want your money. I want you to keep it, or better yet, give it back to the taxpayers."

What I've found over the years is that this approach is often refreshing to legislators. They're used to folks knocking on their office doors requesting public funds for their good cause. Be the person who supports the other approach: "I think we can do better without it." Tom was just at the mission recently with his wife to have a coffee with me, hear about our work, and to personally support the mission. All of that was possible because I took the initiative to build a relationship with him.

Another suggestion is to consider hosting regular meetings to engage your local representatives. I regularly have dinner with a small group of leaders and policymakers. During one of these meals a few years back, I was sharing a problem we were having with our social enterprise endeavor called The Worth Shop. People could come to our mission to earn what they needed by working at The Worth Shop—most of which were short and simple tasks, like a thirty-minute craft or basic chores. By law, we were required to cover them with workers' compensation insurance. Why? According to state law, they were considered employees even though they didn't receive a paycheck.

After describing this problem and the cost-prohibitive nature of the current law, I suggested some additional language for an upcoming workers' compensation bill. Thanks to building relationships with local representatives over these regular dinners, Senate Bill 1 was passed into law in 2014 to modify the definition of an employee: "The act stipulates that 'employee' shall not include any person performing services for board, lodging, aid, or sustenance received from any religious, charitable or relief organization."[3]

Another time I had dinner with a Mississippi legislator who asked me to share my experiences with a caucus working on welfare reform. I made the trip to Mississippi in 2016 and shared some of the experiences (including some that you've read in this book) with a group of legislators who were wrestling with a bill on welfare reform. A year later, the most significant welfare reform bill in Mississippi, House Bill 1090, better known as the HOPE Act, passed into law. Three years later in 2019, I ran into one of those legislators, and he recalled my presentation. "Your talk was a key motivator for us to move forward on that bill." I'm glad I made it a priority to have dinner with that policymaker in 2015 to continue building a network of relationships.

Whether it's your state capitol or our federal capitol, they're just buildings with offices and people in them. They are not kings and queens in castles (even if some may act like it). They are your representatives, and they are human beings just like you—mothers and fathers, brothers and sisters, neighbors and friends. So be courageous by calling ahead to set up an appointment. Make the trip, meet your representatives, share your ideas, and build relationships.

SERVE THE CAUSE

Reading to stay abreast on current policy events, writing your opinion about them, and building relationships in the policy space will impact your community. Can you go a step further and serve the cause? You're reading this book because you care about the poor and you care about freedom. There are policy think tanks and congressional caucuses who support the same causes and could use your help.

Our True Charity Initiative serves policy think tanks by surveying our network's nonprofit leaders with a current event policy question every month. Their responses are sent on to better inform the policy wonks of the impact that certain policies have on charitable organizations and their efforts.

But you don't have to run an association or nonprofit to serve the policy cause. When you're building those relationships with your city council or congressional leaders, offer your testimony based on your real experiences. I've testified regarding panhandling at the city level, welfare legislation in multiple states, and as a witness in a food stamp reform hearing before a US congressional committee. Your experiences are important, and your willingness to share them is as well.

My willingness to serve the cause of policy reform related to poverty has afforded me several opportunities to address various groups. Recently, I was asked to encourage and remind the staff of a large policy think tank about the importance of their work by connecting their efforts to experiences I have had. It was an honor to remind these committed men and women that their welfare reform work reduces government dependency and helps people have a flourishing life.

During the question and answer time, someone asked me, "Thank you for coming and sharing, but how can we help you?"

I responded, "I need you to crack the nut on welfare data at the city level."

I went on to share that in nearly every state, including my own, welfare data is only published at the county level. In other words, unless you live in Maine (and maybe some other state I'm yet unaware of), you and I have no clear way to determine how many people are using TANF,

SNAP, WIC, or any other acronyms which stand for various federal or state welfare programs. In fact, we don't know how many people are enrolled in our cities, and we don't know how much is spent at the municipal level, either. This means that city leaders, stakeholders, and nonprofit leaders in a city have no knowledge of baseline government dependency. This lack of ground-zero information naturally deters community leaders from developing plans to move that metric. Beyond our counties, we must arm our individual communities with welfare data.

So their team is moving forward with that endeavor. After failed attempts by my state's executive branch to force the Department of Social Services to report this data, there is finally a bill for the upcoming legislative session. As you can guess, I've offered to serve as a witness for this hearing. Whatever your passion or community's need, you can suggest something similar to a think tank or state legislator in your state.

SUPPORT THIS

So what kind of policy reform should we support? Work requirements for able-bodied adults on the food stamp program? Asset testing as part of the income threshold determinant for welfare eligibility? Shortening the length of time a family can receive Temporary Assistance for Needy Families?

None of these are bad ideas, but keep in mind that each of them, as well as many other typical reform ideas, regulate state programs rather than provide a pathway for the private sector to replace state programs.

After testifying in favor of private alternatives to government feeding programs at a US Senate hearing, I was approached by a disgruntled woman who said, "I don't think you should put the burden of feeding people on the backs of charities." I was shocked if not a little offended. She could tell, but doubled down, "I just think it should be government first and charity last."

I think it should be charities first and government last. So, my interest is less in improving the outcomes of state welfare programs and more in bold policies that return the primary rights and responsibility back to the communities who naturally and more intimately understand their situations and needs.

What if we enacted policies that protected subsidiarity?

Imagine a few communities who, by pilot legislation, can defer people seeking welfare to local, private sources. This policy-protected subsidiarity is a charity zone. Rather than welfare being the first form of help, the welfare offices would await a referral from the local, private sector, instead.

Some scoff at the idea of the private sector replacing welfare, but let's gain some perspective. First, the private sector already supports the current welfare state, with less than a third of the taxed "contribution" reaching the person in need.[4] Second, not every welfare program or operation has to be replaced. An upper strata of beneficiaries who barely slip into qualifying for a single program may be the initial target. For example, those in the 120–130 percent poverty line bracket could be deferred from the welfare office to instead seek help at a local food ministry. Finally, typical welfare reforms may show clear metrics on how many people "drop off the rolls," but fail to measure how much of the tab was picked up by local charities. A charity zone plan could trace a specific trail from the initial welfare office where a client was vetted and qualified to the private network where relief and outcomes are tracked. This would provide a new perspective on the power of the private sector to care for the poor and the potential for more compassionate care to replace an overly mechanized welfare system that lacks human touch and fails to inspire hope for a better future.

Another reassuring aspect of this plan is that it doesn't call for the demolition of the welfare system. It simply requires that it be layered according to the natural law of subsidiarity. The safety net remains, but the charity zone plan makes it more of a true "last resort" safety net by giving local communities the first shot to help their neighbors in need.

Once when I was testifying in favor of welfare reform at my state capital, I met a woman from St. Louis who testified in opposition. In the hall afterward, we had a civil debate about food stamps. "Do you attend church anywhere?" I asked. She nodded. "Does your church have a food pantry?" She nodded again. I continued, "Would you rather have a person in need first come to your church or to the welfare office?"

It didn't take her long: "I'd rather see them at the church." That's the beauty of a charity zone plan. It represents the possibility of bridging the political divide by simply protecting subsidiarity without eliminating any of the distant layers of help.

Whether it's pushing for a charity zone plan in DC or discussing with your city councilman better ways to help people off the streets, policy is incredibly weighty in the matter of poverty alleviation. Don't be uninformed. Don't be silent. Don't sit back. Too much is on the line for too many people—those in poverty, you, me, our neighbors, and the future of our nation.

Conclusion

WE SAT TOGETHER, SHARING HOT coffee and small talk. A recent cold snap drove this handful of folks from their homeless encampment to find relief in the foyer of our mission. As we sat, I found myself wishing they would come in off the streets to begin a journey toward a better life. Finally, I asked aloud, "Why not?" I let the silence grow awkward until the truth finally came out: addiction.

Addiction to drugs and alcohol was the primary reason these individuals couldn't—wouldn't—submit to the structured rules required at most shelters and housing ministries. That small group huddled in the warmth beside me was representative of the more than 250,000 people who live on the streets in the US today. Generational poverty, broken families, neglect, trauma, addiction, mental illness, and homelessness are a common path for too many.

As I sipped my coffee, I felt compassion for these three guys and two gals who looked so worn and weathered. But, just like any of us, they each have decisions to make every day, for better or for worse.

Then I thought to flip the question. "Why?" I asked. "Why continue in your addictions and stay on the streets?"

One of the guys perched on a stool said, "I don't know how to live sober."

"Like too much pain?" I asked.

"Yeah. Too much pain," he replied.

One young man sitting on the floor with his legs crossed kept his head down, shaking it like he was wrestling with something. "What is it?" I prodded.

"I just don't know how to stay away from it."

"Stay away from what?"

"Meth."

These folks weren't free. They were anchored to the streets and whatever numbs the pain. Desiring to know what kept them tied to that anchor, I asked, "How? How do you guys keep up the habits with no jobs?"

One woman beside me immediately responded, "We sell our government phones."

Another followed, "Or sell our food stamps at half price."

The woman volleyed, "Of course, panhandling."

This group expressed their dependence on three forms of charity: panhandling (private charity) and government cell phones and food stamps (public charity). After that conversation, as I reflected on their responses, I was reminded again that when our compassion fails, it promotes faulty charity and is complicit in our current crisis of dependency.

Did the legislators feel compassion in 1964 when they cast votes in favor of forming the food stamp program? Probably no less than those who cast votes in favor of the Telecommunications Act in 1996, which provides phone services to people in need by taxing phone companies, who have since burdened consumers with that tax through "universal service fees." And for many, it's compassion that drives a person to roll down his window and hand cash to someone with a cardboard sign that reads, "Anything helps. God bless." Compassion may drive all three forms of charity—free phones, free food, and free cash—but the five in our foyer that day were clear: that kind of charity fuels their addictions and ties them to a life of deep poverty.

Compassion failed.

I heard someone once say, "Man doesn't desire freedom. He desires comfort." Although I understand this, I disagree. I believe man desires both comfort *and* freedom, but that there is a tension between the two: the pursuit of comfort over freedom will eventually result in the loss of both. Comfort is simply easier to attain than freedom is to retain. This is also true in the world of charity. It's easier to comfort people than it is to help them find freedom.

Compassion that only comforts people is complicit in the destruction of lives. When misguided and not coupled with wisdom, compassion fuels a fire of careless charity in policy and practice, which strips people of their dignity, hope, and freedom that will eventually, if not corrected, strip our entire nation of the same.

On the other hand, compassion motivated by the hope for man's freedom has the potential to destroy poverty. It can drive charity toward justice. Rather than trap someone in dependency, it can assist a person toward freedom. We weren't born to be comforted in dependence, but to have agency and purpose, which are only discovered when we're free. If we truly love our neighbors in need, we will respect that same freedom-nature in them.

Charity fails to free when it reinforces learned helplessness through repetitive handouts, or when it creates perverse incentives for a person to remain in a "qualifying bracket" of poverty, or when it encourages someone to continue receiving that charity instead of improving their situation.

Instead, our compassion and the charity it births must respect the God-given gifts and capacity in all people. Every person has intrinsic capabilities, and our job in helping the poor is to recognize them, remind the individual of them, and then develop them. This form of empowerment creates a sustainable pathway out of poverty, unlike entitlement programs that distribute aid and remind the poor of their perpetual want and lack.

This is hard work. More than any other reason, it's hard work because it requires real relationships. Today, there are a great number of people developing plans to help the poor who don't really want to be with the poor. This is an unfortunate personal problem that will bar us from ever solving the social one. That's because poverty is a social problem that can't be solved by social policy. It requires personal involvement.

Our national playbook for poverty is lacking a chapter—the one that requires personal involvement, real relationship development, and, often, sacrifice. Not only are we failing to promote this, but much of our public policy interferes with it! As publicly funded programs to help the poor continue to grow in number and scope, private contribution and personal involvement will continue to be crowded out to the detriment of the poor and our nation. This is the greatest tragedy of all. Over the last century, there has been a gradual but consistent shift of charity's onus from the private sector to the public sector with the hope that government's bounty and power will someday cure poverty.

It hasn't. And it won't, because it can't.

The time is late for the mantle of caring for the poor to be returned to the shoulders of compassionate neighbors, corner churches, and local ministries. As citizens, if we fail to either regain or exercise this rightful responsibility, well, we will fail to retain our freedom. No nation can tax itself enough to lift the poor out of poverty. Private individuals must be compassionately compelled to do the work, using local knowledge and relationships to empower people through relationship, accountability, and work rather than handout charity.

Only then do the poor have a chance to experience life as it "ought to be." And only then will our nation truly be the land of the free.

Challenge Questions

CHAPTER 1

1. Reflect on how "justice" is defined in this chapter. What do you think the difference is between what is "just" and what are "human rights"? Could something be just ("what ought to be") but not be a human right? **Learning Objective (LO): Understand the difference between justice and human rights.**
2. Recall a time you felt real compassion for someone who was hurting. How would you describe your thoughts and feelings about the situation? What actions did you take, and why did you take them? Looking back on the situation now, what would you do differently? **LO: Identify the feelings associated with compassion and how they compel us to act.**
3. Vice and poverty often go hand in hand. Alcohol abuse, nicotine addiction, and objectionable language are vices people regularly have when they arrive at Watered Gardens Ministries. How do you feel about being around people who smoke, drink, or curse? Does that impact your desire to engage with them? **LO: Identify the feelings associated with disgust/judgmentalism and how they may prevent us from acting.**
4. Review the 5 Steps to Dependency and the 5 Steps to Paternalism defined in this chapter. Do you believe it is possible to stop the process at Step 4 ("expectation") and prevent someone from becoming dependent on the aid? For example, imagine that you are volunteering at a food pantry and a person comes in for the

fourth time. What should you do? **LO: Understand the 5 Steps of Dependency/Paternalism and consider if the process is inevitable or if it could be disrupted.**

CHAPTER 2

1. Review the Cycle of Nations discussed in this chapter. At what point in the cycle does the decline begin? Do you believe the cycle is accurate? Why or why not? Do you believe the cycle can be stopped? Why or why not? **LO: Understand the Cycle of Nations and consider if the process is inevitable or if it could be disrupted.**
2. Recall the story shared in this chapter of Kenny, a panhandler who creatively crafted his cardboard sign to appeal to four different types of individuals. **LO: Form an opinion about panhandling, both from a person perspective and as a national issue.**
    a. If you encountered Kenny on the street, would you give him money? Why or why not?
    b. Do you believe something should be done to reduce panhandling in the United States? If no, why not? If yes, what do you think is the best way to address the issue?
3. Consider the term "learned helplessness" defined in this chapter. Now imagine you're sitting with a person who has" learned helplessness" and doesn't believe anything they do will help them escape the poverty they are trapped in. What would you say to them? **LO: Understand the effects of "learned helplessness" and consider an appropriate response.**
4. What would you say to a person who fears making more money because of the risk that his benefits might get reduced? **LO: Understand the effects of the welfare cliff and consider an appropriate response.**
5. Have you known anyone or heard of anyone who feared making more money because it would reduce their government benefits? What do you think the impact of this "welfare cliff" is on anti-poverty efforts? **LO: Understand that the fear of a welfare cliff is real and what its impact is on charity work.**

CHAPTER 3

1. Reflect on how "power" is defined in this chapter. Now consider an impoverished person who enters a mission like Watered Gardens. They often need food, shelter, and clothing, and they feel powerless. Is it possible for the mission to supply their basic needs while at the same time helping them develop a sense of power over their own lives? Why or why not? **LO: Understand why care and attention is needed in charity so as to not undermine the power/agency of the people in need.**
2. Think about a time that you had to overcome a challenge—this could be a physical challenge like physical therapy or a mental challenge like at school or work. **LO: Relate to an impoverished individual by understanding the need for healthy challenges.**
    a. What did you need to overcome that challenge?
    b. How empowering did it feel to overcome that challenge?
    c. How can overcoming challenges help an impoverished person gain empowerment?
3. If your goal is to empower people who are currently impoverished, why is it better to help a person earn and create value through their own work than to sign them up for various government aid programs? In your own words, how would you explain why self-reliance is more empowering than dependency? **LO: Confidently explain why empowerment through work is better than dependency.**

CHAPTER 4

1. Consider the last time you helped an acquaintance or a stranger. What was his need? Could a government program (real or imagined) meet that same need? What would become of the challenges or limitations of creating such a government program? **LO: Understand how government programs often do the same things as private charities on a small scale.**
2. Imagine you won $100 million in a lottery. What charitable efforts would you want to help fund with your new wealth? **LO: Under-**

stand how government programs often do the same things as private charities on a large scale.
   a. Those efforts you identified—are there government programs that already exist to meet those needs?
   b. How would your charitable efforts be better than the government's programs?
3. Do you believe that there are ever circumstances when the government should handle charity rather than private individuals, churches, or nonprofit organizations? When and how would you define that threshold? **LO: Consider when government action is appropriate and how most current government action does not meet that threshold.**
4. Imagine that you volunteer at a food pantry, and someone tells you that your activities there are unnecessary because there are government programs to feed people. What would you say to that person? **LO: Learn to overcome objections about private charitable work and articulate why private charity is superior to government aid.**

CHAPTER 5

	RARELY		OCCASIONALLY		FREQUENTLY
I feel valued by society.	1	2	3	4	5
I attend local community events.	1	2	3	4	5
I visit with my neighbors.	1	2	3	4	5
I feel at home in my community.	1	2	3	4	5
I talk with people outside of my family.	1	2	3	4	5
I talk on the phone with people outside of my family.	1	2	3	4	5
I eat outside my house with people who aren't family.	1	2	3	4	5
I have guests inside my home, who aren't family.	1	2	3	4	5
I spend time with my friends in their homes.	1	2	3	4	5
I have close friends.	0-1	2-3	3-4	4-5	>5

1. At Watered Gardens we use this assessment to measure "social capital" (as defined in this chapter). Take the assessment yourself.

Add up your score and see how much social capital you have.
Results:
< 20 = Impoverished Social Capital
20–29 = Low Social Capital
30–31 = Average Social Capital
> 40 = Abundant Social Capital

For reference, the typical person at our mission scores about 25 points on this assessment.

How do you interpret your results? **LO: Understand what makes up social capital and how it impacts their lives as well as the typical people at a mission.**

2. Consider a government program that provides for a need that, to some extent, might be met through neighborly volunteer help. How do you think that affects relationships between neighbors? Does it limit social capital for the recipients of the aid? If so, how? **LO: Understand how government programs often crowd out private charity and limit social capital building on a small scale.**

3. Imagine that you were asked to help meet a need for someone who wasn't in your family, and you find out that they have family members who could help meet that need but aren't. Do you think that if you stepped in and met the need that you would be relieving some responsibility of the person's family? How would that impact that person's family relationships? In this situation, how could you ensure your help doesn't crowd out someone else's charity? **LO: Recognize that most crowding-out is well-intentioned and consider how it can be reduced in our own charitable efforts.**

CHAPTER 6

1. When you consider volunteer opportunities, do you think of them as a chance to be *with* people in need, or to *do something* for people in need? What do you think the main differences are between the two positions? **LO: Understand the importance of being "with" people and how it is different from simply "doing for" people.**

2. Do you know someone who is passionate about freedom but lacks compassion for others? How would you characterize that individual's behavior? **LO: Recognize the disordered behavior that results from an over-emphasis on freedom without compassion for people.**
3. Can you think of a person who has compassion for others, but doesn't care about freedom? What do you think motivates that individual? **LO: Recognize the disordered behavior that results from excessive compassion for people without an appropriate emphasis on freedom.**
4. Character, hard work, and mutual trust are just a few of the components of a flourishing life discussed in this chapter. What would you add to this list? **LO: Articulate why the journey from poverty to a flourishing life is a series of processes that can't be circumvented by simply meeting material needs.**
    a. Is your list made up of material goods or intangible goods (i.e., spiritual and emotional processes)?
    b. Looking at your list, how would you define the journey out of poverty in your own words?

CHAPTER 7

1. Many nonprofit organizations rely on government funding to run their poverty alleviation programs. This chapter discussed several problems and challenges that result from a charity accepting government funds. What would you say to someone working at a nonprofit who wants to move away from its own dependency on government funding but doesn't know how? **LO: Understand why some nonprofit organizations rely on government funding even though they know the risks, and articulate why they should seek to stop their dependence on government funds.**
2. Imagine that someone asks you the following question: "Isn't it exploitation of the poor to make them work for what they need?" How would you respond? **LO: Learn to overcome a common**

objection to charities who involve the recipient in the process of earning their aid.
3. This chapter lays out three main areas in which charity workers can improve their work: Authentic Charity (charity that is voluntarily funded), Accurate Charity (charity that involves the recipient), and Actualized Charity (charity that is focused on outcomes). **LO: Understand the importance of Authentic, Accurate, and Actualized charity and why these are difficult, but worthwhile goals.**
    a. Which of these three areas surprised you the most?
    b. Which of these three areas do you think is the most overlooked?
    c. Which of these three areas do you think is the hardest for charities to implement?

CHAPTER 8

1. Imagine yourself in the role of a philanthropist. Would you anticipate negative outcomes from funding a nonprofit that requires nothing of its clients? Explain what your specific concerns would be. **LO: Understand what some of the unintended negative consequences are of charitable work that requires nothing of its recipients.**
2. Continuing to imagine yourself in the role of a philanthropist, how would you respond if an organization that you were funding began receiving a large amount of government grant money? Would you continue to fund them? What questions would you have for them about how your funds were being used? **LO: Understand how government funds can crowd out private charity from the perspective of a philanthropist.**
3. This chapter emphasized the importance of supporting organizations that measure the actual outcomes of their charitable work. There are a mix of "outputs" and "outcomes" in the list below. Place them in order of importance to you. Explain your reasoning. **LO: Understand the difference between "outputs" and "outcomes" and correctly differentiate between examples of both.**

- » Number of vocational certificates earned from a long-term residential program
- » Number of people served at a clothing bank
- » Pounds of food distributed from a church food pantry
- » Graduation rate in a recovery program
- » Percent of people employed from a shelter
- » Number of families who achieve independent housing

4. Why do you think some donors do not care to ask the questions in this chapter or get involved with the charitable causes they fund? **LO: Consider that some philanthropists may be motivated by other reasons than actual societal change (i.e., tax write-offs, prestige, virtue signaling, etc.)**

CHAPTER 9

1. Make a list of the top three reasons why people in the United States are disengaging from the political process. Which one do you believe is the most impactful? Explain why. **LO: Consider the factors that are causing Americans to disengage from the political process.**
2. This chapter discusses a bill in the state of Missouri that would require welfare statistics to be reported at the community level, rather than the county level. If this happened in your state, how would you use that information to serve the cause of poverty alleviation in your community? **LO: Understand the local impact of poverty-related legislation.**
3. Review the concept of a "charity zone" discussed in this chapter. If this happened in your area, what portion of the current welfare benefits being received in your community do you think private charities, including churches, could replace? **LO: Think through the impact of a creative policy solution such as a charity zone.**
    a. What hurdles would need to be overcome to make the charity zone as successful as possible?
    b. How would a charity zone benefit the current welfare recipients in your community?

Acknowledgments

ON MARCH 12, 2020, MY wife and I celebrated twenty years of marriage in a hot air balloon, silently floating over the farmlands of Delaware. When we landed, the silence ended. Covid was making its way to the US and panic gripped people around the globe. The pandemic required a tremendous amount of effort and sacrifice from the entire team at our mission, Watered Gardens, in Joplin, Missouri. Rather than close our doors, we continued to serve the most vulnerable and marginalized, doing all we could to mitigate the spread of a deadly virus without neglecting those who were impoverished and homeless.

That team showed more grit and selflessness than I've ever seen in a group before, and their determination to press on under a unique set of pressures inspired my own determination to pick this small book project up again after a year of lying dormant.

Last year, more than 3,000 volunteers served at our mission. That compassionate, beautiful commitment to give a portion of one's life away to another has been the source of growth for our ministry over the last twenty-five years. Without them, this book would be mostly blank pages.

I also want to acknowledge the team at True Charity. Their passion and determination to champion a resurgence of civil society in the fight against poverty has not only blessed me but has given me much to admire and write about. Many years ago, my wife and I dreamed of a day when handout charity would be replaced with compassionate, relational, effective forms of help. The team at True Charity is leading the way.

There are four founders who have been a great source of inspiration: Marvin Olasky, who co-founded Zenger House; Ismael Hernandez, who founded the Freedom and Virtue Institute; Kris Mauren, who co-founded the Acton Institute; and Tarren Bragdon, who founded the Foundation for Government Accountability. At the time of this publication, each of these men continue to lead their organizations. Their common love of God and tireless pursuit of truth as well as their passionate, clarion, and sometimes prophetic voices have spurred me on in the causes of charity, liberty, and justice.

Finally, and most importantly, I want to acknowledge my wife and children. They have extended much grace over the years as long days of ministry bled into the twilight hours. *The Crisis of Dependency* was part of that "extra" and they have given it with me. To my wife, Marsha, especially, who founded our ministry with me nearly twenty-five years ago, I am especially grateful. She has modeled well what's needed for the change we all want to see—compassion.

References

CHAPTER 1
1. Social Justice, Socialism, and Democracy, 3 Austrian Lectures by F.A. Hayek. Accessed August 12, 2024, https://www.cis.org.au/wp-content/uploads/2015/07/op2.pdf
2. Ken Wytsma, *Pursuing Justice: The Call to Live and Die for Bigger Things* (Nashville: Thomas Nelson, 2013), 8.
3. Robert D. Lupton, *Toxic Charity: How Churches and Charities Hurt Those They Help and How to Reverse It* (New York: HarperOne, 2011), 130.
4. Marvin Olasky, *The Tragedy of American Compassion* (Washington, D.C.: Regnery Publishing, 1994), 112.

CHAPTER 2
1. The Heritage Foundation, "United States," *2022 Index of Economic Freedom*, accessed July 2, 2022, https://www.heritage.org/index/pages/country-pages/united-states.
2. Office of Management and Budget, Efficient, Effective, Accountable. An American Budget. Fiscal Year 2019." February 11, 2018, accessed August 7, 2022, https://www.govinfo.gov/content/pkg/BUDGET-2019-BUD/pdf/BUDGET-2019-BUD.pdf, 119.
3. Donald S. Hiroto and Martin E. P. Seligman, "Generality of Learned Helplessness in Man," *Journal of Personality and Social Psychology* 31, no. 2 (1975): 311-327, accessed October 13, 2022, https://www.appstate.edu/~steelekm/classes/psy5150/Documents/Hiroto&Seligman1975-learned-helplessness.pdf.
4. The Foundation for Government Accountability, "Waivers Gone Wild: How States Are Still Fostering Dependency," p.25, accessed July 31, 2024, https://thefga.org/research/work-requirement-waivers-gone-wild/.
5. Federal Reserve Bank of America, "Benefits Cliffs Across the U.S." Missouri, Greene County, accessed July 22, 2024, https://emar-data-tools.shinyapps.io/prd_dashboard/

CHAPTER 3
1. See Watered Gardens in the introduction.

2. Foundation for Government Accountability, *April's Story*, 2017, accessed July 2, 2022, https://www.youtube.com/watch?v=mt4gIG57d68.
3. Lord Acton, "Letter to Archbishop Mandell Creighton," April 5, 1887, accessed July 2, 2022, https://history.hanover.edu/courses/excerpts/165acton.html.
4. Don Davis, "Amazon Is the Fourth-largest US Delivery Service and Growing Fast," Digital Commerce 360, May 26, 2020, accessed July 2, 2022, https://www.digitalcommerce360.com/2020/05/26/amazon-fourth-largest-us-delivery-service/.
5. Annie Palmer, "Amazon Poised to Pass UPS and FedEx to Become Largest U.S. Delivery Service by Early 2022, Exec Says," CNBC, November 29, 2021, accessed July 2, 2022, https://www.cnbc.com/2021/11/29/amazon-on-track-to-be-largest-us-delivery-service-by-2022-exec-says.html.
6. Saul Venskutonis, "Is Jeff Bezos Becoming Too Powerful?," Quora, accessed July 2, 2022, https://www.quora.com/Is-Jeff-Bezos-becoming-too-powerful.
7. "Education | Povertycure," accessed July 2, 2022, https://www.povertycure.org/learn/issues/human-person/education.
8. "Moving On Up: Why Do Some Americans Leave the Bottom of the Economic Ladder, but Not Others?" Pew Charitable Trust, November 2013, accessed July 7, 2022, https://www.pewtrusts.org/~/media/assets/2013/11/01/movingonuppdf.pdf.
9. Alexis de Tocqueville, Seymour Drescher, and Gertrude Himmelfarb, *Alexis de Tocqueville's Memoir on Pauperism* (London: IEA Health and Welfare Unit, 1997), accessed July 2, 2022, http://www.civitas.org.uk/pdf/Tocqueville_rr2.pdf.
10. "OAT & Outcomes | SOAR Works!," accessed July 2, 2022, https://soarworks.samhsa.gov/about-the-model/oat-and-outcomes.
11. "Annual Statistical Supplement, 2018 - OASDI Current-Pay Benefits: Disabled Workers," accessed July 2, 2022, https://www.ssa.gov/policy/docs/statcomps/supplement/2018/5d.pdf.
12. John Locke, "The Two Treatises of Civil Government (Hollis Ed.)," Online Library of Liberty, accessed July 2, 2022, https://oll.libertyfund.org/title/hollis-the-two-treatises-of-civil-government-hollis-ed#Lock_0057_255.
13. Frédéric Bastiat, *The Law* (Irvington-on-Hudson, New York: The Foundation for Economic Education Inc, 1850), accessed July 2, 2022, http://bastiat.org/en/the_law.html.
14. Hayden Dubois, Jonathan Bain, and Jonathan Ingram, "Food Stamp Work Requirements Worked for Missourians," The Foundation for Government Accountability, accessed October 13, 2022, https://thefga.org/paper/missouri-food-stamp-work-requirements/.

CHAPTER 4

1. Catherine C. Eckel, Philip J. Grossman, and Rachel M. Johnston, "An Experimental Test of the Crowding out Hypothesis," *Journal of Public Economics*, The Experimental Approaches to Public Economics, 89, no. 8 (August 1, 2005): 1543–60, accessed July 2, 2022, https://doi.org/10.1016/j.jpubeco.2004.05.012.
2. Jonathan Gruber and Daniel M. Hungerman, "Faith-Based Charity and Crowd-out during the Great Depression," *Journal of Public Economics* 91, no. 5 (June 1, 2007): 1043–69, accessed July 2, 2022, https://doi.org/10.1016/j.jpubeco.2006.11.004.
3. U.S. Trust and Lilly Family School of Philanthropy, "The 2014 U.S. Trust Study of High Net Worth Philanthropy," accessed July 2, 2022, https://www

.privatebank.bankofamerica.com/publish/content/application/pdf/GWMOL/USTp_ARNTCJF5_2015-11_vi.pdf

4. "CAF World Giving Index 2018," Charities Aid Foundation (October 2018), accessed July 3, 2022, https://www.cafonline.org/docs/default-source/about-us-publications/caf_wgi2018_report_webnopw_2379a_261018.pdf.
5. Benedict XVI, *Caritas in Veritate*, 2009, para. 6, accessed July 3, 2022, https://www.vatican.va/content/benedict-xvi/en/encyclicals/documents/hf_ben-xvi_enc_20090629_caritas-in-veritate.html.
6. James Madison, Appendix to "Congressional Record and Appendix, Forty-Third Congress, First Session," 1874, p. 195, https://www.google.com/books/edition/Congressional_Record/G7hiAAAAcAAJ?hl=en&gbpv=1&dq=1794+house+of+representatives+debate+madison+charity+is+no+part+of+ the+legislative+duty+of+the+government&pg=PA195&printsec=frontcover
7. Grover Cleveland, "Veto of Texas Seed Bill," Miller Center, February 16, 1887, accessed July 3, 2022, https://millercenter.org/the-presidency/presidential-speeches/february-16-1887-veto-texas-seed-bill.
8. William Taft, "Message Regarding Income Tax," Miller Center, June 16, 1909, accessed July 3, 2022, https://millercenter.org/the-presidency/presidential-speeches/june-16-1909-message-regarding-income-tax
9. Edward T. Devine, "Pensions for Mothers," *The Survey: Vol. XXX* (New York: Survey Associates, Inc, 1913), 459, accessed July 3, 2022, https://archive.org/details/surveycharityorg30survrich/page/458/mode/2up
10. Daniel J. Smith and Daniel Sutter, "Response and Recovery after the Joplin Tornado: Lessons Applied and Lessons Learned," *SSRN Electronic Journal*, 2013, https://doi.org/10.2139/ssrn.2261353.
11. Howie Gordon, "Joplin Salvation Army Funding Cuts," *KSNF/KODE - FourStatesHomepage.com* (blog), August 4, 2016, accessed October 13, 2022, https://www.fourstateshomepage.com/news/joplin-salvation-army-funding-cuts/.
12. Natalee Kasza, "Filling in the Gaps: How Job-Readiness Programs Equip Guests for Workplace Success," *Instigate*, July/August 2019, 14-15.
13. Aristotle, *Politics, Book Two*, translated by Benjamin Jowett, para. 10, accessed July 3, 2022, http://classics.mit.edu/Aristotle/politics.2.two.html.
14. Cleveland, "Veto of Texas Seed Bill."

CHAPTER 5

1. Robert D. Putnam, *Bowling Alone: Revised and Updated: The Collapse and Revival of American Community* (New York: Simon and Schuster, 2020), 22-23.
2. Xavier de Souza Briggs, "Brown Kids in White Suburbs: Housing Mobility and the Many Faces of Social Capital," *Housing Policy Debate*, 1998, 179.
3. Ibid, 205.
4. "Shelter Plus Care Resource Manual," May 2002, 11, accessed July 3, 2022, https://files.hudexchange.info/resources/documents/Shelter-Plus-Care-Resource-Manual.pdf
5. Eric Laverentz, *Is Caesar Our Savior? Why Only the Church Can Keep Any Nation Free* (Lee's Summit, MO: Father's Press, LLC 2012), 174.
6. "Breadlines," Encyclopedia of the Great Depression, Encyclopedia.com,

accessed July 3, 2022, https://www.encyclopedia.com/economics/encyclopedias-almanacs-transcripts-and-maps/breadlines.
7. Ronald Fowler and Amy Henchey, "In-Kind Contributions," n.d., accessed July 3, 2022, https://www.irs.gov/pub/irs-tege/eotopice94.pdf.
8. Alexis de Tocqueville, *Alexis de Tocqueville's Memoir on Pauperism,* translated by Seymour Drescher (London: IEA Health and Welfare Unit, 1997), 31, accessed July 3, 2022, http://www.civitas.org.uk/pdf/Tocqueville_rr2.pdf.

CHAPTER 7

1. Arthur C. Brooks. *The Conservative Heart: How to Build a Fairer, Happier, and More Prosperous America.* HarperCollins. Kindle Edition, p. 66.
2. Center for Poverty and Inequality Research, University of California, Davis, accessed August 17, 2024, https://poverty.ucdavis.edu/faq/what-deep-poverty,
3. Pius XI, *Quadragesimo Anno,* 1931, para. 79, accessed July 3, 2022, https://www.vatican.va/content/pius-xi/en/encyclicals/documents/hf_p-xi_enc_19310515_quadragesimo-anno.html.

CHAPTER 8

1. Niall McCarthy, "The Development Of America's Homeless Population," Statista Infographics, April 16, 2021, accessed July 3, 2022, https://www.statista.com/chart/24642/total-number-of-homeless-people-in-the-us-by-year/.
2. Adam Smith, *An Inquiry Into the Nature and Causes of the Wealth of Nations,* (London: T. Nelson, 1852), 6.
3. Jordan Larimore, "Donations to Local Mission Limited by IRS Rules," *The Joplin Globe*, May 16, 2018, accessed July 3, 2022, https://www.joplinglobe.com/news/local_news/donations-to-local-mission-limited-by-irs-rules/article_abf2a470-196a-5cde-b926-27b826a57167.html.
4. "Publication 526 (2021), Charitable Contributions," Internal Revenue Service, accessed July 3, 2022, https://www.irs.gov/publications/p526.
5. Our True Charity Initiative offers training and tools to help nonprofits and churches improve their effectiveness.
6. Giving USA, accessed July 28, 2024, https://givingusa.org/wp-content/uploads/2021/06/GUSA2021_Infographic_Digital.pdf

CHAPTER 9

1. Aristotle, *Politics, Book One,* Section 1253a, accessed July 3, 2022, http://www.perseus.tufts.edu/hopper/text?doc=Perseus:abo:tlg,0086,035:1:1253a.
2. John Stuart Mill, *On Liberty* (Mineola, NY: Dover Publications, 2002), 39.
3. "SB1 - Modifies the Law Relating to Workers' Compensation," January 1, 2014, accessed July 3, 2022, http://senate.mo.gov/13info/BTS_Web/Bill.aspx?SessionType=R&BillID=16944728.
4. James Rolph Edwards, "The Costs of Public Income Redistribution and Private Charity,"*Journal of Libertarian Studies* 21, no. 2 (Summer 2007): 3-20, accessed July 3, 2022, https://cdn.mises.org/21_2_1.pdf.

www.ingramcontent.com/pod-product-compliance
Lightning Source LLC
Chambersburg PA
CBHW070159100426
42743CB00013B/2973